THE DOCTRINES

AND

DISCIPLINE

OF THE

METHODIST EPISCOPAL CHURCH.

1876.

WITH AN APPENDIX.

NEW YORK:
NELSON & PHILLIPS.
CINCINNATI:
HITCHCOCK & WALDEN.

Entered according to Act of Congress, in the year 1876, by
NELSON & PHILLIPS,
In the Office of the Librarian of Congress at Washington.

EPISCOPAL ADDRESS.

To the Members of the Methodist Episcopal Church:

Dearly Beloved Brethren: We think it expedient to give you a brief account of the rise of Methodism, both in Europe and America. "In 1729 two young men in England, reading the Bible, saw they could not be saved without holiness: followed after it, and incited others so to do. In 1737 they saw, likewise, that men are justified before they are sanctified: but still holiness was their object. God then thrust them out to raise a holy people." These are the words of John and Charles Wesley.

In the year 1766 Philip Embury, a Wesleyan Local Preacher from Ireland, began to preach in the city of New York, and formed a Society of his own countrymen and the citizens;

and the same year, Thomas Webb, a captain in the British army, and also a Wesleyan Local Preacher, preached in a hired room near the barracks. About the same time Robert Strawbridge, another Local Preacher from Ireland, settled in Frederick County, in the State of Maryland, and preaching there, formed some Societies. The first Methodist Church built in America was erected in New York in 1768. In 1769 Richard Boardman and Joseph Pilmoor, two itinerant Wesleyan Preachers of England, were sent to America by Mr. Wesley. These were the first Methodist Traveling Preachers on the Continent. In the latter end of the year 1771 Francis Asbury and Richard Wright, of the same country and order, were sent over.

We believe that God's design in raising up the Methodist Episcopal Church in America was, to reform the continent and spread Scriptural holiness over these lands. As a proof hereof, we have seen since that time a great and glorious work of God extending throughout all the United States and Territories, and throughout the British possessions of North America; and the planting of successful missions in South America and in Mexico. Moreover, the Methodist Episcopal Church, in its organic form as well as spiritual power, has been successfully planted in Africa, Asia, and Europe, and God has given her great prosperity in those countries.

We esteem it our duty and privilege most earnestly to recommend to *you*, as members of our Church, our FORM OF DISCIPLINE, which has been founded on the experience of a long series of years, as also on the observations and remarks we have made on ancient and modern Churches.

We wish this little publication may be found in the house of every Methodist, and the more so as it contains the Articles of Religion, maintained more or less, in part or in whole, by every reformed Church in the world.

Far from wishing you to be ignorant of any of our Doctrines, or any part of our Discipline, we desire you to read, mark, learn, and inwardly digest the whole. You ought, next to the Holy Scriptures, to understand the Articles of Religion and the Rules of the Church to which you belong.

We remain your very affectionate Brethren and Pastors,

EDMUND S. JANES,
LEVI SCOTT,
MATTHEW SIMPSON,
EDWARD R. AMES,
THOMAS BOWMAN,
WILLIAM L. HARRIS,
RANDOLPH S. FOSTER,
ISAAC W. WILEY,
STEPHEN M. MERRILL,
EDWARD G. ANDREWS,
GILBERT HAVEN,
JESSE T. PECK.

NOTE.—In the head lines of the following pages the No. of the paragraphs (¶) therein contained is shown by placing on the left hand page the *first* No. on the page, on the right hand page the *last* No.; thus showing all the paragraphs contained on the two pages facing each other.—EDITOR.

CONTENTS

PART I.

Origin, Doctrines, and Rules.

CHAPTER I.

ORIGIN, ARTICLES OF RELIGION, AND GENERAL RULES.

CHAPTER II.

THE MEMBERSHIP OF THE CHURCH.

CHAPTER III.

MEANS OF GRACE.

PART II.

Government of the Church.

CHAPTER I.

THE CONFERENCES.

CHAPTER II.

THE MINISTRY.

CHAPTER III.

STEWARDS.

PART III.

Administration of Discipline.

CHAPTER I.

BRINGING MINISTERS AND MEMBERS TO TRIAL, AND THE SETTLEMENT OF DISPUTES.

CHAPTER II.

TRIAL OF APPEALS.

CHAPTER III.

RESTORATION OF CREDENTIALS OF ORDINATION.

PART IV.

Educational and Benevolent Institutions.

PART V.

Temporal Economy.

CHAPTER I.

SUPPORT OF MINISTERS.

CHAPTER II.

RAISING SUPPLIES—PARSONAGES.

CHAPTER III.

CHURCHES AND CHURCH PROPERTY.

CHAPTER IV.

BOUNDARIES OF CONFERENCES.

PART VI.

Ritual of the Church.

APPENDIX.

DOCTRINES AND DISCIPLINE

OF THE

METHODIST EPISCOPAL CHURCH.

PART I.

ORIGIN, DOCTRINES, AND RULES.

CHAPTER I.

ORIGIN, ARTICLES OF RELIGION, AND GENERAL RULES.

Origin of the Methodist Episcopal Church.

¶ **1.** The preachers and members of our Society in general, being convinced that there was a great deficiency of vital religion in the Church of England in America, and being in many places destitute of the Christian Sacraments, as several of the clergy had forsaken their Churches, requested the late Rev. John Wesley to take such measures, in his wisdom and prudence, as would afford them suitable relief in their distress.

¶ **2.** In consequence of this, our venerable friend, who, under God, had been the father of the great revival of religion now extending over the earth by the means of the Methodists, determined to ordain Ministers for America; and for this purpose, in the year 1784, sent over three regularly-ordained clergymen; but, preferring the episcopal mode of Church government to any other, he solemnly set apart, by the imposition of his hands and prayer, one of them, namely, Thomas Coke, Doctor of Civil Law, late of Jesus College, in the University of Oxford, and a Presbyter of the Church of England, for the episcopal office; and having delivered to him letters of episcopal orders, commissioned and directed him to set apart Francis Asbury, then General Assistant of the Methodist Society in America, for the same episcopal office, he, the said Francis Asbury, being first ordained Deacon and Elder. In consequence of which the said Francis Asbury was solemnly set apart for the said episcopal office by prayer, and the imposition of the hands of the said Thomas Coke, other regularly-ordained ministers assisting in the sacred ceremony. At which time the General Conference, held at Baltimore, did unanimously receive the said THOMAS COKE and FRANCIS ASBURY as their Bishops, being fully satisfied of the validity of their episcopal ordination.

ARTICLES OF RELIGION.

I. *Of Faith in the Holy Trinity.*

¶ **3.** There is but one living and true God, everlasting, without body or parts, of infinite power, wisdom, and goodness; the maker and preserver of all things, visible and invisible. And in unity of this Godhead there are three persons, of one substance, power, and eternity, the Father, the Son, and the Holy Ghost.

II. *Of the Word, or Son of God, who was made very Man.*

¶ **4.** The Son, who is the Word of the Father, the very and eternal God, of one substance with the Father, took man's nature in the womb of the blessed Vir gin; so that two whole and perfect natures, that is to say, the Godhead and manhood, were joined together in one person, never to be divided, whereof is one Christ, very God and very man, who truly suffered, was crucified, dead and buried, to reconcile his Father to us, and to be a sacrifice, not only for original guilt, but also for the actual sins of men.

III. *Of the Resurrection of Christ.*

¶ 5. Christ did truly rise again from the dead, and took again his body, with all things appertaining to the perfection of man's nature, wherewith he ascended into heaven, and there sitteth until he return to judge all men at the last day.

IV. *Of the Holy Ghost.*

¶ 6. The Holy Ghost, proceeding from the Father and the Son, is of one substance, majesty, and glory with the Father and the Son, very and eternal God.

V. *The Sufficiency of the Holy Scriptures for Salvation.*

¶ 7. The Holy Scriptures contain all things necessary to salvation; so that whatsoever is not read therein, nor may be proved thereby, is not to be required of any man that it should be believed as an article of faith, or be thought requisite or necessary to salvation. In the name of the Holy Scripture we do understand those canonical books of the Old and New Testament of whose authority was never any doubt in the Church. The names of the canonical books are—

Genesis, Exodus, Leviticus, Numbers, Deuteronomy, Joshua, Judges, Ruth, The First Book of Samuel, The Second Book of Samuel, The First Book of Kings, The Second Book of Kings, The First Book of Chronicles, The Second Book of Chronicles, The Book of Ezra, The Book of Nehemiah, the Book of Esther, the Book of Job, The Psalms, The Proverbs, Ecclesiastes or the Preacher, Cantica or Songs of Solomon, Four Prophets the greater, Twelve Prophets the less.

All the books of the New Testament, as they are commonly received, we do receive and account canonical.

VI. *Of the Old Testament.*

¶ 8. The Old Testament is not contrary to the New; for both in the Old and

New Testament everlasting life is offered to mankind by Christ, who is the only Mediator between God and man, being both God and man. Wherefore they are not to be heard who feign that the old fathers did look only for transitory promises. Although the law given from God by Moses, as touching ceremonies and rites, doth not bind Christians, nor ought the civil precepts thereof of necessity be received in any commonwealth; yet, notwithstanding, no Christian whatsoever is free from the obedience of the commandments which are called moral.

VII. *Of Original or Birth Sin.*

¶ **9.** Original sin standeth not in the following of Adam, (as the Pelagians do vainly talk,) but it is the corruption of the nature of every man, that naturally is engendered of the offspring of Adam, whereby man is very far gone from original righteousness, and of his own nature inclined to evil, and that continually.

VIII. *Of Free Will.*

¶ **10.** The condition of man after the fall of Adam is such that he cannot turn and prepare himself, by his own natural strength and works, to faith, and calling upon God; wherefore we have no power to do good works, pleasant and acceptable to God, without the grace of God by Christ preventing us, that we may have a good will, and working with us, when we have that good will.

IX. *Of the Justification of Man.*

¶ **11.** We are accounted righteous before God only for the merit of our Lord and Saviour Jesus Christ by faith, and not for our own works or deservings. Wherefore, that we are justified by faith only, is a most wholesome doctrine, and very full of comfort.

X. *Of Good Works.*

¶ **12.** Although good works, which are the fruits of faith, and follow after justification, cannot put away our sins, and endure the severity of God's judgments; yet are they pleasing and acceptable to God in Christ, and spring out of a true and lively faith, insomuch that by them a lively faith may be as evidently known as a tree is discerned by its fruit.

XI. *Of Works of Supererogation.*

¶ **13.** Voluntary works—besides, over, and above God's commandments—which are called works of supererogation, cannot be taught without arrogancy and impiety. For by them men do declare that they do not only render unto God as much as they are bound to do, but that they do more for his sake than of bounden duty is required: whereas Christ saith plainly, When ye have done all that is commanded you, say, We are unprofitable servants.

XII. *Of Sin after Justification.*

¶ **14.** Not every sin willingly committed after justification is the sin against the Holy Ghost, and unpardonable. Wherefore, the grant of repentance is not to be denied to such as fall into sin after justification: after we have received the Holy Ghost, we may depart from grace given, and fall into sin, and, by the grace of God, rise again and amend our lives. And therefore they are to be condemned who say they can no more sin as long as they live here; or deny the place of forgiveness to such as truly repent.

XIII. *Of the Church.*

¶ **15.** The visible Church of Christ is a congregation of faithful men, in which the pure word of God is preached, and the sacraments duly administered, according to Christ's ordinance, in all those things that of necessity are requisite to the same.

XIV. *Of Purgatory.*

¶ **16.** The Romish doctrine concerning purgatory, pardon, worshiping and adoration, as well of images as of relics, and also invocation of saints, is a fond thing, vainly invented, and grounded upon no warrant of Scripture, but repugnant to the word of God.

XV. *Of Speaking in the Congregation in such a Tongue as the People understand.*

¶ **17.** It is a thing plainly repugnant to the word of God, and the custom of the primitive Church, to have public prayer in the Church, or to minister the sacraments, in a tongue not understood by the people.

XVI. *Of the Sacraments.*

¶ **18.** Sacraments ordained of Christ are not only badges or tokens of Christian men's profession, but rather they are certain signs of grace, and God's good will toward us, by the which he doth work invisibly in us, and doth not only quicken, but also strengthen and confirm, our faith in him.

There are two sacraments ordained of Christ our Lord in the Gospel; that is to say, Baptism and the Supper of the Lord.

Those five commonly called sacraments, that is to say, confirmation, penance, orders, matrimony, and extreme unction, are not to be counted for sacraments of the Gospel; being such as have partly grown out of the *corrupt* following of the apostles, and partly are states of life allowed in the Scriptures, but yet have not the like nature of Baptism and the Lord's Supper, because they have not any visible sign or ceremony ordained of God.

The sacraments were not ordained of Christ to be gazed upon, or to be carried about; but that we should duly use them. And in such only as worthily receive the same, they have a wholesome effect or operation: but they that receive them unworthily, purchase to themselves condemnation, as St. Paul saith, 1 Cor. xi, 29.

XVII. *Of Baptism.*

¶ **19.** Baptism is not only a sign of profession, and mark of difference, whereby Christians are distinguished from others that are not baptized; but it is also a sign of regeneration, or the new birth. The baptism of young children is to be retained in the Church.

XVIII. *Of the Lord's Supper.*

¶ **20.** The Supper of the Lord is not only a sign of the love that Christians ought to have among themselves one to another, but rather is a sacrament of our redemption by Christ's death; insomuch that, to such as rightly, worthily, and with faith receive the same, the bread which we break is a partaking of the body of Christ; and likewise the cup of blessing is a partaking of the blood of Christ.

Transubstantiation, or the change of the substance of bread and wine in the Supper of our Lord, cannot be proved by Holy Writ, but is repugnant to the plain words of Scripture, overthroweth the nature of a sacrament, and hath given occasion to many superstitions.

The body of Christ is given, taken, and eaten in the Supper, only after a heavenly and spiritual manner. And the means whereby the body of Christ is received and eaten in the Supper, is faith.

The sacrament of the Lord's Supper was not by Christ's ordinance reserved, carried about, lifted up, or worshiped.

XIX. *Of both Kinds.*

¶ 21. The cup of the Lord is not to be denied to the lay people; for both the parts of the Lord's Supper, by Christ's ordinance and commandment, ought to be administered to all Christians alike.

XX. *Of the one Oblation of Christ, finished upon the Cross.*

¶ 22. The offering of Christ, once made, is that perfect redemption, propitiation, and satisfaction for all the sins of the whole world, both original and actual;

and there is none other satisfaction for sin but that alone. Wherefore the sacrifice of masses, in the which it is commonly said that the priest doth offer Christ for the quick and the dead, to have remission of pain or guilt, is a blasphemous fable and dangerous deceit.

XXI. *Of the Marriage of Ministers.*

¶ **23.** The ministers of Christ are not commanded by God's law either to vow the estate of single life, or to abstain from marriage: therefore it is lawful for them, as for all other Christians, to marry at their own discretion, as they shall judge the same to serve best to godliness.

XXII. *Of the Rites and Ceremonies of Churches.*

¶ **24.** It is not necessary that rites and ceremonies should in all places be the same, or exactly alike; for they have been always different, and may be changed according to the diversity of countries, times, and men's manners, so that nothing be ordained against God's word. Whosoever, through his private judgment, willingly and purposely doth openly break the rites and ceremonies of the

Church to which he belongs, which are not repugnant to the word of God, and are ordained and approved by common authority, ought to be rebuked openly, that others may fear to do the like, as one that offendeth against the common order of the Church, and woundeth the consciences of weak brethren.

Every particular Church may ordain, change, or abolish rites and ceremonies, so that all things may be done to edification.

XXIII. *Of the Rulers of the United States of America.*

¶ **25.** The President, the Congress, the General Assemblies, the Governors, and the Councils of State, *as the delegates of the people*, are the rulers of the United States of America, according to the division of power made to them by the Constitution of the United States, and by the Constitutions of their respective States. And the said States are a sovereign and independent nation, and ought not to be subject to any foreign jurisdiction.*

* As far as it respects civil affairs, we believe it the duty of Christians, and especially all

XXIV. *Of Christian Men's Goods.*

¶ **26.** The riches and goods of Christians are not common, as touching the right, title, and possession of the same, as some do falsely boast. Notwithstanding, every man ought of such things as he possesseth, liberally to give alms to the poor, according to his ability.

XXV. *Of a Christian Man's Oath.*

¶ **27.** As we confess that vain and rash swearing is forbidden Christian men by our Lord Jesus Christ and James his apostle; so we judge that the Christian religion doth not prohibit, but that a man may swear when the magistrate requireth, in a cause of faith and charity, so it be done according to the prophet's teaching, in justice, judgment, and truth.

Christian ministers, to be subject to the supreme authority of the country where they may reside, and to use all laudable means to enjoin obedience to the powers that be; and therefore it is expected that all our preachers and people, who may be under the British or any other government, will behave themselves as peaceable and orderly subjects.

THE GENERAL RULES.

THE NATURE, DESIGN, AND GENERAL RULES OF OUR UNITED SOCIETIES.

¶ 28. In the latter end of the year 1739 eight or ten persons came to Mr. Wesley in London, who appeared to be deeply convinced of sin, and earnestly groaning for redemption. They desired, as did two or three more the next day, that he would spend some time with them in prayer, and advise them how to flee from the wrath to come, which they saw continually hanging over their heads. That he might have more time for this great work, he appointed a day when they might all come together; which from thenceforward they did every week, namely, on *Thursday*, in the evening. To these, and as many more as desired to join with them, (for their number increased daily,) he gave those advices from time to time which he judged most needful for them; and they always concluded their meeting with prayer suited to their several necessities.

¶ 29. This was the rise of the UNITED SOCIETY, first in *Europe*, and then in *America*. Such a society is no other than "*a company of men* having the form and seeking the power of *godliness, united in order to pray together, to receive the word of exhortation, and to watch over one another in love, that they may help each other to work out their salvation.*"

¶ 30. That it may the more easily be discerned whether they are indeed working out their own salvation, each Society is divided into smaller companies, called classes, according to their respective places of abode. There are about twelve persons in a class, one of whom is styled *the Leader*. It is his duty,—

§ 1. To see each person in his class once a week at least; in order, (1.) To inquire how their souls prosper. (2.) To advise, reprove, comfort, or exhort, as occasion may require. (3.) To receive what they are willing to give toward the relief of the Preachers, Church, and poor.*

§ 2. To meet the Ministers and the Stewards of the Society once a week; in order, (1.) To inform the minister of any that are sick, or of any that walk disorderly, and will not be reproved. (2.) To pay the

* This part refers to towns and cities, where the poor are generally numerous, and church expenses considerable.

Stewards what they have received of their several classes in the week preceding.

¶ 31. There is only one condition previously required of those who desire admission into these Societies, "a desire to flee from the wrath to come, and to be saved from their sins." But wherever this is really fixed in the soul, it will be shown by its fruits.

¶ 32. It is therefore expected of all who continue therein, that they should continue to evidence their desire of salvation,—

First, by doing no harm, by avoiding evil of every kind, especially that which is most generally practiced; such as,—

The taking of the name of God in vain.

The profaning the day of the Lord, either by doing ordinary work therein or by buying or selling.

Drunkenness, buying or selling spirituous liquors, or drinking them, unless in cases of extreme necessity.

Slaveholding; buying or selling slaves.

Fighting, quarreling, brawling, brother going to law with brother; returning evil for evil, or railing for railing; the using many words in buying or selling.

The buying or selling goods that have not paid the duty.

The giving or taking things on usury, that is, unlawful interest.

Uncharitable or unprofitable conversation; particularly speaking evil of magistrates or of ministers.

Doing to others as we would not they should do unto us.

Doing what we know is not for the glory of God; as,—

The putting on of gold and costly apparel.

The taking such diversions as cannot be used in the name of the Lord Jesus.

The singing those songs, or reading those books, which do not tend to the knowledge or love of God.

Softness and needless self-indulgence.

Laying up treasure upon earth.

Borrowing without a probability of paying; or taking up goods without a probability of paying for them.

¶ 33. It is expected of all who continue in these Societies that they should continue to evidence their desire of salvation,—

Secondly, By doing good; by being in every kind merciful after their power; as they have opportunity, doing good of every possible sort, and, as far as possible, to all men:

To their bodies of the ability which God giveth, by giving food to the hungry, by clothing the naked, by visiting or helping them that are sick or in prison:

To their souls, by instructing, reproving, or exhorting all we have any intercourse with; trampling under foot that enthusiastic doctrine, that "we are not to do good unless *our hearts be free to it.*"

By doing good, especially to them that are of the household of faith, or groaning so to be; employing them preferably to others, buying one of another, helping each other in business; and so much the more because the world will love its own and them *only.*

By all possible *diligence* and *frugality,* that the Gospel be not blamed.

By running with patience the race which is set before them, *denying themselves, and taking up their cross daily;* submitting to bear the reproach of Christ, to be as the filth and offscouring of the world, and looking that men should say *all man ner of evil of them falsely for the Lord's sake.*

¶ 34. It is expected of all who desire to continue in these Societies that they should continue to evidence their desire of salvation,—

Thirdly, By attending upon all the ordinances of God; such are,—

The public worship of God:

The ministry of the word, either read or expounded:

The Supper of the Lord:

Family and private prayer:

Searching the Scriptures:

Fasting or abstinence.

¶ 35. These are the General Rules of our Societies; all which we are taught of God to observe, even in his written word, which is the only rule, and the sufficient rule, both of our faith and practice. And all these we know his Spirit writes on truly awakened hearts. If there be any among us who observes them not, who habitually breaks any of them, let it be known unto them who watch over that soul as they who must give an account. We will admonish him of the error of his ways. We will bear with him for a season. But if then he repent not, he hath no more place among us. We have delivered our own souls.

Slavery.

¶ 36. We declare that we are as much as ever convinced of the great evil of Slavery. We believe that the buying, selling, or holding of human beings, to be used as chattels, is contrary to the laws of God and nature, and inconsistent with the Golden Rule, and with that rule in our Discipline which requires all who desire to continue among us to "do no harm," and to "avoid evil of every kind." We therefore affectionately admonish all our preachers and people to keep themselves pure from this great evil, and to seek its extirpation by all lawful and Christian means.

Baptism.

¶ 37. Let every adult person, and the parents of every child to be baptized, have the choice either of immersion, sprinkling, or pouring.

¶ 38. We will on no account whatever

make a charge for administering baptism, or for burying the dead.

The Lord's Supper.

¶ 39. Let persons who have scruples concerning the receiving of the Lord's Supper kneeling, be permitted to receive it either standing or sitting.

¶ 40. No person shall be admitted to the Lord's Supper among us who is guilty of any practice for which we would exclude a member of our Church.

Rules Relating to Marriage.

¶ 41. Many of our members have married with *unawakened* persons. This has produced bad effects; they have been either hindered for life, or have turned back to perdition.

¶ 42. To discourage such marriages, 1. Let every Preacher publicly enforce the apostle's caution, "Be ye not unequally yoked together with unbelievers." 2 Cor. vi, 14. 2. Let all be exhorted to take no step in so weighty a matter without advising with the more serious of their brethren.

¶ 43. In general a woman ought not to marry without the consent of her parents. Yet there may be exceptions. For if, 1. A woman believe it to be her duty to marry: if, 2. Her parents absolutely refuse to let her marry any Christian: then she may, nay, ought to marry without their consent. Yet even then a Methodist preacher ought not to be married to her.

¶ 44. We do not prohibit our people from marrying persons who are not of our Church, provided such persons have the form, and are seeking the power, of godliness; but we are determined to discourage their marrying persons who do not come up to this description.

Concerning Dress.

45. We should by all means insist on the rules concerning dress. This is no time to encourage superfluity in dress. Therefore, let all our people be exhorted to conform to the spirit of the apostolic precept, not to adorn themselves "with gold, or pearls, or costly array," 1 Tim. ii, 9.

PART I.—CHAPTER II.

THE MEMBERSHIP OF THE CHURCH.

Receiving Members into the Church

¶ 46. In order to prevent improper persons from insinuating themselves into the Church,—

§ 1. Let no one be received into the Church until such person has been at least six months on trial, and has been recommended by the Leaders and Stewards' Meeting, or where no such meeting is held, by the Leader, and has been baptized; and shall, on examination by the Minister in Charge before the Church, give satisfactory assurances both of the correctness of his faith and of his willingness to observe and keep the rules of the Church.* Never theless, if a member in good standing in any other orthodox Church shall desire

* Persons baptized in infancy must publicly assent, before the Church, to the Baptismal Covenant. The re-baptism of persons known to have been previously baptized is inconsistent with the nature and design of baptism as set forth in the New Testament.

to unite with us, such applicant may, by giving satisfactory answers to the usual inquiries, be received at once into full fellowship.

§ 2. Let none be admitted on trial except they are well recommended by one you know, or until they have met twice or thrice in class.

§ 3. Read the Rules to them the first time they meet.

¶ 47. That we may be more exact in receiving and excluding members, the Preacher in Charge shall, at every Quarterly Meeting, read the names of those that are received into the Church, and also of those that are excluded therefrom.

The Relation of Baptized Children to the Church.

¶ 48. We hold that all children, by virtue of the unconditional benefits of the atonement, are members of the kingdom of God, and, therefore, graciously entitled to baptism; but as infant baptism contemplates a course of religious instruction and discipline, it is expected of all parents or guardians who present their children for baptism, that they use all diligence in bringing them up in conformity to the word of God; and they should be solemnly admonished of this obligation, and earnestly exhorted to faithfulness therein.

¶ **49.** We regard all children who have been baptized as placed in visible covenant relation to God, and under the special care and supervision of the Church.

¶ **50.** The Preacher in Charge shall preserve a full and accurate register of the names of all the baptized children within his pastoral care; the dates of their birth, baptism, their parentage, and places of residence.

¶ **51.** The Preacher in Charge shall organize the baptized children of the Church, at the age of ten years or younger, into classes, and appoint suitable leaders, (male or female,) whose duty it shall be to meet them in class once a week, and instruct them in the nature, design, and obligations of baptism, and the truths of religion necessary to make them "wise unto salvation;" urge them to give regular attendance upon the means of grace; advise, exhort, and encourage them to an immediate consecration of their hearts and lives to God, and inquire into the state of their religious experience; *provided*, that children unbaptized are not to be excluded from these classes.

¶ **52.** Whenever baptized children shall have attained an age sufficient to understand the obligations of religion, and shall give evidence of piety, they may be admitted into full membership in our Church, on the recommendation of a Leader with whom they have met at least six months in class, by publicly assenting before the Church to the Baptismal Covenant, and also to the usual questions on Doctrines and Discipline.

¶ **53.** Whenever a baptized child shall, by orphanage or otherwise, become deprived of Christian guardianship, the Preacher in Charge shall ascertain and report to the Leaders and Stewards' Meeting the facts in the case; and such provision shall be made for the Christian training of the child as the circumstances of the case admit and require.

PART I.—CHAPTER III.

MEANS OF GRACE.

Public Worship.

¶ 54. For the establishment of uniformity in public worship among us on the Lord's day:—

§ 1. Let the morning service consist of singing, prayer, the reading of a lesson from the Old Testament, and another from the New, and preaching.

§ 2. Let the afternoon or evening service consist of singing, prayer, the reading of one or two Scripture lessons, and preaching.

§ 3. On the days of administering the sacrament of the Lord's Supper, the reading of the Scripture lessons may be omitted.

§ 4. In administering the sacraments, and in the burial of the dead, let our form of Ritual invariably be used. Let the Lord's Prayer also be used on all occasions of public worship in concluding the first prayer, the congregation being exhorted to join in its audible repetition. Let a Doxology be sung at the conclusion of each service, and the Apostolic benediction be invariably used in dismissing the congregation.

§ 5. Let the people be earnestly exhorted to take part in the public worship of God—first, in singing; secondly, in prayer, in the scriptural attitude of kneeling, by the repetition of the Lord's Prayer.

§ 6. Let the Society be met, wherever it is practicable, on the Sabbath day.

The Spirit and Truth ot Singing.

¶ **55.** To guard against formality in singing:—

§ 1. Choose such hymns as are proper for the occasion, and do not sing too much at once; seldom more than four or five verses.

§ 2. Let the tune be suited to the sentiment, and do not suffer the people to sing too slowly.

§ 3. In every Society let due attention be given to the cultivation of sacred music.

§ 4. Should the Preacher in Charge desire it, let the Quarterly Conference appoint annually a committee of three or more, who, co-operating with him, shall regulate all matters relating to this part of divine worship.

§ 5. As singing is a part of divine worship in which all ought to unite, therefore exhort every person in the congregation to sing, not one in ten only.

Classes and Class-Meetings.

¶ 56. The design of the organization of classes and the appointment of Leaders is,—

§ 1. To establish a system of pastoral oversight that shall effectively reach every member of the Church.

§ 2. To establish and keep up a meeting for social and religious worship, for instruction, encouragement, and admonition, that shall be a profitable means of grace to our people.

§ 3. To carry out, unless other measures be adopted, a financial plan for the raising of moneys.

¶ 57. The primary object of distributing the members of the Church into classes is to secure the sub-pastoral oversight made necessary by our itinerant economy. In order to secure this oversight,—

§ 1. Let a report of the condition of his Class be presented by the Leader at each meeting of the Quarterly Conference.

§ 2. Let each Leader be careful to inquire how every soul of his Class prospers; not only how each person outwardly observes the rules, but how he grows in the knowledge and love of God.

§ 3. Let the Leaders converse with those who have the charge of their Circuits and Stations frequently and freely.

¶ **58.** In order to render our class-meetings interesting and profitable, 1. Remove improper Leaders. 2. See that all the Leaders be not only men of sound judgment, but men truly devoted to God.

¶ **59.** In the arrangement of Class-meetings two or more Classes may meet together, and be carried on according to such plan as shall be agreed upon by the Leaders in concurrence with the Preacher in Charge.

¶ **60.** Let care be observed that they do not fall into formality through the use of a uniform method. Let speaking be voluntary or the exercises conversational, the Leader taking such measures as may best assist in making the services fresh, spiritual, and of permanent religious profit.

¶ **61.** Let the Leaders be directed to such a course of reading and study as shall best qualify them for their work; especially let such books be recommended as will tend to increase their knowledge of the Scriptures and make them familiar with those passages best adapted to Christian edification. Whenever practicable, let the Preachers examine the Leaders in the studies recommended.

PART II.

GOVERNMENT OF THE CHURCH.

CHAPTER I.

THE CONFERENCES.

The General Conference.

¶ 62. The General Conference shall be composed of Ministerial and Lay Delegates. The Ministerial Delegates shall consist of one member for every forty-five members of each Annual Conference, to be appointed either by seniority or choice at the discretion of such Annual Conference, yet so that such representatives shall have traveled at least four full calendar years from the time that they were received on trial by an Annual Conference, and are in full connection at the time of holding the Conference.*

* A Transferred Preacher shall not be counted twice in the same year in the basis of the election of Delegates to the General Conference, nor vote for Delegates to the General Confer-

¶ **63.** The Lay Delegates shall consist of two laymen for each Annual Conference, except such Conferences as have but one Ministerial Delegate, which Conferences shall be entitled to one Lay Delegate each.

¶ **64.** The Lay Delegates shall be chosen by an Electoral Conference of Laymen, which shall assemble for the purpose on the third day of the session of the Annual Conference, at the place of its meeting, at its session immediately preceding the General Conference.

¶ **65.** The Electoral Conference shall be composed of one Layman from each Circuit or Station within the bounds of the Annual Conference, such laymen to be chosen by the last Quarterly Conference preceding the time of the assembling of such Electoral Conference; and on assembling, the Electoral Conference shall organize by electing a Chairman and Secretary of their own number; *provided*, that no Layman shall be chosen a Delegate either to the Electoral Conference

ence in any Annual Conference where he is not counted as a part of the basis of representation, nor vote twice the same year on any constitutional question.

or to the General Conference who shall be under twenty-five years of age, or who shall not have been a member of the Church in full connection for the five consecutive years preceding the elections.*

¶ **66.** The General Conference shall meet on the first day of May, in the year of our Lord 1812, in the City of New York, and thenceforward on the first day of May once in four years perpetually, in such place or places as shall be fixed on by the General Conference from time to time; but the General Superintendents, or a majority of them, by or with the advice of two thirds of all the Annual Conferences, or, if there be no General Superintendent, two thirds of all the Annual Conferences, shall have power to call an extra session of the General Conference at any time, to be constituted in the usual way.

* The Secretaries of the several Annual and Electoral Conferences shall send to the Secretary of the last General Conference a certified copy of the election of Delegates and Reserves to the next General Conference, in the order of their election, as soon after the election as practicable, so that a roll of Members and Reserves may be prepared for the opening of the next General Conference.

¶ **67.** At all times when the General Conference is met it shall take two thirds of the whole number of Ministerial and Lay Delegates to form a quorum for transacting business.

¶ **68.** The Ministerial and Lay Delegates shall sit and deliberate together as one body, but they shall vote separately whenever such separate vote shall be demanded by one third of either order; and in such cases the concurrent vote of both orders shall be necessary to complete an action.

¶ **69.** One of the General Superintendents shall preside in the General Conference; but in case no General Superintendent be present, the General Conference shall choose a president *pro tem.*

¶ **70.** The General Conference shall have full powers to make rules and regulations for our Church, under the following limitations and restrictions, namely:—

§ 1. The General Conference shall not revoke, alter, or change our Articles of Religion, nor establish any new standards or rules of doctrine contrary to our present existing and established standards of doctrine.

§ 2. They shall not allow of more than

one Ministerial Representative for every fourteen members of the Annual Conference, nor allow of a less number than one for every forty-five, nor more than two Lay Delegates for any Annual Conference; *provided*, nevertheless, that when there shall be in any Annual Conference a fraction of two thirds the number which shall be fixed for the ratio of representation, such Annual Conference shall be entitled to an additional Delegate for such fraction; and *provided*, also, that no Conference shall be denied the privilege of one Delegate.

§ 3. They shall not change or alter any part or rule of our government, so as to do away Episcopacy, or destroy the plan of our itinerant General Superintendency; but may appoint a Missionary Bishop or Superintendent for any of our foreign missions, limiting his jurisdiction to the same respectively.

§ 4. They shall not revoke or change the General Rules of the United Societies.

§ 5. They shall not do away the privileges of our ministers or preachers, of trial by a Committee, and of an appeal; neither shall they do away the privileges of our members, of trial before the

Society, or by a Committee, and of an appeal.

§ 6. They shall not appropriate the produce of the Book Concern, nor of the Charter Fund, to any purpose other than for the benefit of the traveling, supernumerary, superannuated, and worn-out preachers, their wives, widows, and children.

¶ **71.** *Provided*, nevertheless, that upon the concurrent recommendation of three fourths of all the members of the several Annual Conferences who shall be present and vote on such recommendation, then a majority of two thirds of the General Conference succeeding shall suffice to alter any of the above restrictions, excepting the First Article; and also, whenever such alteration or alterations shall have been first recommended by two thirds of the General Conference, so soon as three fourths of the members of all the Annual Conferences shall have concurred as aforesaid, such alteration or alterations shall take effect.

The Annual Conferences.

¶ **72.** There shall be eighty-nine Annual Conferences in the year, and these shall severally become bodies corporate, wherever practicable, under the authority of the laws of the States and Territories within whose bounds they are located.

¶ **73.** All the Traveling Preachers, both those who are in full connection and those who are on trial, shall attend the Annual Conferences.

¶ **74.** The Bishops shall appoint the times of holding the Annual Conferences; but they shall allow each Annual Conference to sit a week at least.

¶ **75.** Each Annual Conference shall appoint the place of its own sitting; but should it become necessary, from any unforeseen cause, to change the place of its sitting after it has been fixed by the Conference, the Preacher or Preachers in Charge in the place where the Conference was to have been held, and the Presiding Elder of the District, shall have power to make such change. But this authority shall not be exercised without first consulting the other Presiding Elders of the Conference so far as practicable.

¶ **76.** A Bishop shall preside in the Annual Conferences. In case no Bishop be present, a member of the Conference, appointed by the Bishop, shall preside. But if no appointment be made, or the person appointed do not attend, the Conference shall elect a President by ballot from among the Elders without debate.

¶ **77.** The business of the Annual Conference is, to inquire,—

1. Have any entered this Conference by Transfer or Re-admission?
2. Who are admitted on Trial?
3. Who remain on Trial?
4. Who are admitted into Full Connection?
5. Who are the Deacons of the First Class?
6. Who are the Deacons of the Second Class?
7. Who have been elected and ordained Elders?
8. Who are the Supernumerary Preachers?
9. Who are the Superannuated Preacners?
10. Was the character of each Preacher examined?
11. Have any Located?

12. Have any Withdrawn?

13. Have any been Transferred, and to what Conference?

14. Have any been Expelled?

15. Have any Died?

16. What is the Statistical Report?

(1.) Membership—Number of Probationers. Number of full Members. Number of Local Preachers. Number of Deaths.

(2.) Baptisms—Children. Adults.

(3.) Church Property—Number of Churches. Probable Value. Number of Parsonages. Probable Value. * Amount raised for the Building and Improving Churches and Parsonages. * Present Indebtedness.

(4.) Benevolent Collections—For Conference Claimants: for Missions—from Churches, from Sabbath-schools: for Woman's Foreign Missionary Society: for Board of Church Extension: for Sunday-school Union of the Methodist Episcopal Church: for Tract Society: for Freedmen's Aid Society: for Education: for American Bible Society.

(5.) Sabbath-schools — Number of Schools. Number of Officers and Teachers. Total Number of Scholars of all ages.

* Number of Scholars fifteen years of age and over.

* Number of Scholars under fifteen, except Infant Class.

* Number of Scholars in Infant Class.

* Average Attendance of Teachers and Scholars in whole school.

* Number of Library Books.

* Total Expenses of School this year.

* Number of *Sunday-School Advocates* taken.

* Number of *Sunday-School Journals* taken.

* Number of Officers and Teachers who are Church-members or Probationers.

* Number of Scholars who are Church-members or Probationers.

* Number of Conversions this year.

* (6.) Ministerial Support — Claims. Receipts.

17. What are the Claims upon the Conference Fund?

18. What has been received on the foregoing claims, and how has it been applied?

19. Where are the Preachers stationed?

20. Where and when shall the next Conference be held?

* 21. Have any Local Preachers been ordained ?

* 22. Are any of our Literary or Theological Institutions under the control and patronage of this Conference, and what is their condition ?

*23. Who are the Conference Board of Church Extension ?

[NOTE.—The items marked with a * are not to be included in the General Minutes.]

¶ 78. The Electing and Ordaining of Deacons and Elders is to be done in the Annual Conferences.

¶ 79. It shall be the duty of each Annual Conference to examine strictly into the state of the Domestic Missions within its bounds, and to allow none to remain on the list of its missions which, in the judgment of the Conference, is able to support itself.

¶ 80. Each Annual Conference shall report through its Secretary, annually, to the Secretaries of the Missionary Society at New York, the name of each District, Circuit, or Station, within its bounds, sustained in whole or in part by said Conference as a mission, together with the amount of missionary money appropriated to such for the year, and also the number of years that each Mission has received assistance from the Missionary Treasury, and whether consecutively or otherwise.

¶ **81.** Each Annual Conference shall cause the collections, as reported by the Preachers for the Statistical Tables, to be compared with the receipts of the Conference Treasurers of the several benevolent Societies, that discrepancies, if any, may be corrected before the publication of the Minutes.

¶ **82.** Preachers in Charge shall report to their Annual Conferences as collections actual cash receipts only, and shall hand the money, or a satisfactory voucher for the same, to the Conference Treasurers, otherwise no credit shall be given to a contributing Charge.

¶ **83.** Each Annual Conference shall report, through its Secretary, to the Sunday-School Union, the number of schools within its bounds, together with other facts named in the form published by the Union, and contained in the annual reports of Preachers, as directed in ¶ 175, § 14.

¶ **84.** A record of the proceedings of each Annual Conference shall be kept by a Secretary chosen for the purpose, and shall be signed by the President and Secretary; and a copy of said record shall be sent to the General Conference. Also the minutes and documents of the trial of any member of the Conference who may have been condemned or censured, shall be forwarded with the record.

The District Conferences.

¶ 85. The District Conferences shall be composed of the Traveling and Local Preachers, the Exhorters, the District Stewards, and one Sunday-school Superintendent and one Class Leader from each pastoral Charge in the District. But if there shall be more than one Sunday-school Superintendent in any Circuit or Station, then the Quarterly Conference shall designate one of them for this service, and it shall also select the Class Leader.

¶ 86. The District Conference shall meet once or twice each year in each Presiding Elder's District, as each District Conference shall determine for itself, at such time and place as the Presiding Elder shall designate for the first meeting after the adoption of this plan by the

District; but the District Conference shall at each meeting determine the place for its next meeting, the time to be fixed by the Presiding Elder.

¶ **87.** A Bishop, when present, shall preside at the District Conference. If no Bishop be present, the Presiding Elder of the District shall preside. And if both be absent, the District Conference shall choose its own President by ballot from among the Traveling Elders.

¶ **88.** A record of the proceedings of each District Conference shall be kept by a Secretary chosen for the purpose, and a copy of said record shall be sent to the ensuing Annual Conference.

¶ **89.** The regular business of the District Conference shall be:—

§ 1. To take the general oversight of all the temporal and spiritual affairs of the District, subject to the provisions of the Discipline.

§ 2. To take cognizance of all the Local Preachers and Exhorters in the District, and to inquire respecting the gifts, labors, and usefulness of each by name, and to arrange a plan of appointments for each until the next District Conference.

§ 3. To hear complaints against Local

Preachers: to try, suspend, deprive of ministerial office and credentials, expel or acquit, any Local Preacher against whom charges may be preferred.

§ 4. To license Local Preachers, to renew the licenses of Local Preachers and Exhorters annually, and to recommend to the Annual Conference Local Preachers as suitable candidates for Deacons, or Elders' orders, and for admission on trial in the traveling connection, *provided* that no person shall be licensed to preach, nor shall his license to preach or exhort be renewed, nor shall he be recommended for orders or for admission in the traveling connection, without the recommendation of the Quarterly Conference, or of the Leaders and Stewards' Meeting of the Circuit or Station of which he is a member: and in all cases the candidate shall first pass a satisfactory examination in such course of studies as the Bishops shall prescribe. The District Conference shall also have the powers given to the Quarterly Conference in ¶ 152, § 1, and ¶ 153, relating to the recognition of orders.

§ 5. To inquire whether all the collections for the benevolent institutions of the Church, as recognized by the Discipline, are properly attended to in all the Circuits and Stations, and to adopt suitable measures for promoting their success.

§ 6. To inquire into the condition of the Sunday-schools in the District, and to adopt suitable measures for insuring their success.

§ 7. To inquire respecting opportunities for Missionary and Church Extension enterprises within the District, and to take measures for the occupation of any neglected portion of its territory by Mission Sunday-schools, and by appointments for public worship.

§ 8. To provide for appropriate religious and literary exercises during the sessions, for the mutual benefit of those attending upon them.

¶ 90. The order of business of the District Conference shall be,—

1. To inquire what members of the District Conference are present.
2. To appoint committees on,—
   (1.) Examination of candidates for license to preach.
   (2.) Examination of Local Preachers in each of the four years of the Course of Study.
   (3.) Examination of candidates for

admission into the Traveling Connection.

(4.) Examination of candidates for orders.

(5.) Home Mission work.

(6.) Appointments of Local Preachers and Exhorters.

(7.) Apportionment to each charge of the amounts to be raised for benevolent purposes.

(8.) Programme of religious and literary exercises for next meeting.

(9.) Miscellaneous matters.

8. To receive reports,—

(1.) From the Presiding Elder, as to the condition of the work under his charge, and his own work as Presiding Elder.

(2.) From each Pastor, as to the religious condition of his charge, his pastoral labors, the benevolent collections, and the circulation of our Church periodicals and books.

(3.) From each Local Preacher, the form of which report shall be prescribed by each District Conference.

(4.) From each Exhorter, including a statement of the prayer-meetings he has held, and other work done, especially in destitute places and among the sick and the poor.

(5.) From each District Steward, as to the temporal affairs of the charge he represents.

(6.) From each Superintendent, as to the condition of the Sunday-schools of the charge he represents.

(7.) From each Class Leader as to the condition of the classes of the charge he represents.

(8.) From each Committee.

4. To inquire concerning Local Preachers,—

(1.) Are there any charges or complaints?

(2.) Who shall have their licenses renewed?

(3.) Who shall be licensed to preach?

(4.) Who shall be recommended for ordination?

(5.) Who shall be recommended for recognition of orders?

(6.) Who shall be recommended for admission into the Traveling Connection?

(7.) Where are the Local Preachers stationed?

5. To inquire concerning Exhorters:—
   (1.) Who shall have their licenses renewed?
   (2.) What work is assigned each Exhorter?
6. Where shall the next District Conference be held?
7. Is there any other business?

¶ 91. The order of business may be varied, and the business interspersed with such literary and religious exercises as the Conference may direct.

¶ 92. The provisions for District Conferences shall be of force and binding only in those Districts in which the Quarterly Conferences of a majority of the Circuits and Stations shall have approved the same by asking the Presiding Elder to convene a District Conference, as herein provided. A District Conference may be discontinued by a vote of two thirds of the members present at any regular session, notice thereof having been given at a previous session, and with the concurrence of three fourths of the Quarterly Conferences in the District. In those Districts in which District Conferences shall be held, the powers given to the District Conferences shall not be exercised by the Quarterly Conferences. In all other cases the powers of the Quarterly Conferences shall remain as heretofore provided.

The Quarterly Conferences.

¶ 93. The Quarterly Conferences shall be composed of all the Traveling and Local Preachers, Exhorters, Stewards, Class Leaders, and Trustees, of the Churches in the Circuits or Stations, and the first male Superintendents of our Sunday-schools, said Trustees and Superintendents being members of our Church, and approved by the Quarterly Conference.

¶ 94. The Presiding Elder shall preside in the Quarterly Conferences, and in his absence, the Preacher in Charge shall preside.

¶ 95. The Quarterly Conference shall appoint a Secretary, who shall take minutes of the proceedings thereof, and transmit them to the Recording Steward.

¶ 96. The regular business of the Quarterly Conference shall be,—

§ 1. To hear Complaints, and to receive and try Appeals.

§ 2. To take cognizance of all the Local Preachers and Exhorters in the Circuit or Station, and to inquire into the gifts, labors, and usefulness of each by name; to license proper persons to preach, and renew their license annually, and to recommend the renewal of the license of Exhorters annually when, in the judgment of said Conference, their gifts, grace, and usefulness will warrant such renewal; to recommend to the Annual Conference Local Preachers who are suitable candidates for Deacons' or Elders' orders and for admission on trial in the Traveling Connection; and to try, suspend, deprive of ministerial office and credentials, expel, or acquit, any Local Preacher in the Circuit or Station against whom charges may be preferred; and to receive the annual report of the Trustees. *Provided*, That no person shall be licensed to preach without the recommendation of the Society of which he is a member, or of the Leaders and Stewards' Meeting; nor shall any one be licensed to preach, or recommended to the Annual Conference to travel or for ordination, without first being examined in the Quarterly Conference on the subject of Doctrines and Discipline.

§ 3. To elect Trustees, where the laws of the State permit, and also Stewards, for the Circuit or Station, and of the latter to elect one a District and one a Recording Steward.

§ 4. To have supervision of all the Sunday-schools within the bounds of the Circuit or Station, and to inquire into the condition of each; to approve Trustees not elected by the Quarterly Conference; to approve Sunday-school Superintendents as such, and also as members of the Quarterly Conference; and to remove any Superintendent who may prove unworthy or inefficient.

¶ **97.** The order of business in the respective Quarterly Conferences, after the roll of members has been called and a Secretary appointed, shall be to inquire—

§ 1. AT THE FIRST QUARTERLY CONFERENCE:

1. Who are approved as Trustees? who as Sunday-school Superintendents?
2 Are there any complaints?
3. Are there any appeals?
4. Are there any reports—
   (1.) From the Pastor?
   (2.) From the Class Leaders?
   (3.) From Committees?

5. What amounts have been apportioned to this Charge this year for the support of the Ministry—
   (1.) For the Pastor?
   (2.) For the Assistant?
   (3.) For the Presiding Elder?
   (4.) For the Bishops?
   (5.) For Conference Claimants?
   (6.) For Rent?
   (7.) For Traveling and Moving Expenses?
6. What amounts have been received for the support of the Ministry this Quarter, and how have they been applied?
   Received—
   (1.) For the Preachers and Presiding Elder;
   (2.) For the Bishops;
   (3.) For Rent;
   (4.) For Traveling and Moving Expenses.
   Applied—
   (1.) To the Pastor;
   (2.) To the Assistant;
   (3.) To the Presiding Elder;
   (4.) To the Bishops;
   (5.) On Rent;
   (6.) On Traveling and Moving Expenses.

7. What amounts have been apportioned to this Charge this year for Benevolent Purposes?
   (1.) For Missions?
   (2.) For Church Extension?
   (3.) For Freedmen's Aid Society?
   (4.) For Education?
   (5.) For Tract Society?
   (6.) For Sunday-School Union?
   (7.) Miscellaneous?
8. Are the Sunday-Schools organized into Missionary Societies?
9. Is any change desired in the Board of Stewards?
10. Are there any recommendations for license to preach?
11. Have the General Rules been read this Quarter?
12. Have the Rules respecting the instruction of children been observed?
13. Are the Church Records properly kept?
14. Where and when shall the next Quarterly Conference be held?
15. Is there any other business?

§ 2. AT THE SECOND AND AT THE THIRD QUARTERLY CONFERENCES.

1. Who are approved as Trustees? who as Sunday-school Superintendents?
2. Are there any Complaints?
3. Are there any Appeals?
4. Are there any Reports—
   (1.) From the Pastor?
   (2.) From the Class Leaders?
   (3.) From Committees?
5. What amounts have been received for the support of the Ministry this Quarter, and how have they been applied?

   Received—
   (1.) For the Preachers and Presiding Elder;
   (2.) For the Bishops;
   (3.) For Rent;
   (4.) For Traveling and Moving Expenses.

   Applied—
   (1.) To the Pastor;
   (2.) To the Assistant;
   (3.) To the Presiding Elder;
   (4.) To the Bishops;
   (5.) On Rent;
   (6.) On Traveling and Moving Expenses.

6. Are the Sunday-schools organized into Missionary Societies ?
7. Is any change desired in the Board of Stewards ?
8. Are there any recommendations for license to preach ?
9. Have the General Rules been read this Quarter ?
10. Have the Rules respecting the instruction of children been observed ?
11. Are the Church Records properly kept ?
12. Where and when shall the next Quarterly Conference be held ?
13. Is there any other business ?

§ 3. AT THE FOURTH QUARTERLY CONFERENCE.

1. Who are approved as Trustees? who as Sunday-school Superintendents?
2. What Committees shall be appointed ?
3. Are there any Complaints ?
4. Are there any Appeals ?
5. Are there any Reports?
   (1.) From the Pastor ?
   (2.) From the Class Leaders ?
   (3.) From Trustees ?
   (4.) From Committees ?

6. What amounts have been received for the support of the Ministry this Quarter, and how have they been applied?

Received—

(1.) For the Preachers and Presiding Elder;

(2.) For the Bishops;

(3.) For Conference Claimants;

(4.) For Rent;

(5.) For Traveling and Moving Expenses;

Applied—

(1.) To the Pastor;

(2.) To the Assistant;

(3.) To the Presiding Elder;

(4.) To the Bishops;

(5.) To Conference Claimants;

(6.) On Rent;

(7.) On Traveling and Moving Expenses.

7. What amounts have been raised for Benevolent Purposes this year?

(1.) For Missions?

a. From Churches and Congregations?

b. From Sunday-Schools?

(2.) For Woman's Foreign Missionary Society?

(3.) For Church Extension ?
(4.) For Freedmen's Aid Society ?
(5.) For Education ?
(6.) For Tract Society ?
(7.) For Sunday-School Union ?
(8.) Miscellaneous ?

8. Are the Sunday-schools organized into Missionary Societies ?
9. Who shall be the Stewards for the ensuing Conference year ?
10. Who shall be the Recording Steward ?
11. Who shall be the District Steward ?
12. Who are the Trustees of Church and Parsonage property ?
13. Are there any recommendations for license to preach ?
14. Are there any recommendations of Local Preachers for orders ?
15. Are there any recommendations for admission into the Traveling Connection ?
16. Are there any recommendations for the recognition of orders ?
17. Has the character of the Local Preachers and Exhorters been examined, and have their licenses been renewed ?

18. Have the General Rules been read this Quarter?
19. Have the Rules respecting the instruction of children been observed?
20. Are the Church Records properly kept?
21. Where and when shall the next Quarterly Conference be held?
22. Is there any other business?

¶ **98.** Committees ordered to be appointed by the Quarterly Conference. On Missions. On Sunday-schools. On Tracts. On Education. On Church Extension. On Church Records. On Parsonages and Furniture. On Church Music. On Estimating the Preachers' Salaries. On Estimating the Amount Necessary for Conference Claimants.

PART II.—CHAPTER II.

THE MINISTRY.

The Examination of those who think they are moved by the Holy Ghost to Preach.

¶ 99. In order that we may try those who profess to be moved by the Holy Ghost to preach, let the following questions be asked, namely:—

§ 1. Do they know God as a pardoning God? Have they the love of God abiding in them? Do they desire nothing but God? And are they holy in all manner of conversation?

§ 2. Have they gifts (as well as grace) for the work? Have they (in some tolerable degree) a clear, sound understanding; a right judgment in the things of God; a just conception of salvation by faith? And has God given them any degree of utterance? Do they speak justly, readily, clearly?

§ 3. Have they fruit? Are any truly convinced of sin, and converted to God, by their preaching?

¶ 100. As long as these three marks

concur in any one, we believe he is called of God to preach. These we receive as sufficient proof that he is moved by the Holy Ghost.

Rules for a Preacher's Conduct

¶ **101.** *Rule* 1. Be diligent. Never be unemployed: never be triflingly employed. Never trifle away time; neither spend any more time at any place than is strictly necessary.

¶ **102.** *Rule* 2. Be serious Let your motto be, *Holiness to the Lord.* Avoid all lightness, jesting, and foolish talking.

¶ **103.** *Rule* 3. Converse sparingly, and conduct yourself prudently, with women. (1 Tim. v, 2.)

¶ **104.** *Rule* 4. Take no step toward marriage without first advising with your brethren.

¶ **105.** *Rule* 5. Believe evil of no one without good evidence; unless you see it done, take heed how you credit it. Put the best construction on every thing. You know the judge is always supposed to be on the prisoner's side.

¶ **106.** *Rule* 6. Speak evil of no one; because your word, especially, would eat as doth a canker. Keep your thoughts within your own breast till you come to the person concerned.

¶ **107.** *Rule* 7. Tell every one under your care what you think wrong in his conduct and temper, and that lovingly and plainly, as soon as may be: else it will fester in your heart. Make all haste to cast the fire out of your bosom.

¶ **108.** *Rule* 8. Avoid all affectation. A preacher of the Gospel is the servant of all.

¶ **109.** *Rule* 9. Be ashamed of nothing but sin.

¶ **110.** *Rule* 10. Be punctual. Do every thing exactly at the time. And do not mend our rules, but keep them; not for wrath, but conscience' sake.

¶ **111.** *Rule* 11. You have nothing to do but to save souls, therefore spend and be spent in this work; and go always not only to those that want you, but to those that want you most.

¶ **112.** Observe! it is not your business only to preach so many times, and to take care of this or that Society, but to save as many as you can; to bring as many sinners as you can to repentance, and with a'l your power to build them up in that holiness without which they cannot see the Lord. And remember! a Methodist preacher is to mind every point, great and small, in the Methodist Discipline! Therefore you will need to exercise all the sense and grace you have.

¶ 113. *Rule* 12. Act in all things not according to your own will, but as a son in the Gospel. As such, it is your duty to employ your time in the manner in which we direct: in preaching, and visiting from house to house; in reading, meditation, and prayer. Above all, if you labor with us in the Lord's vineyard, it is needful you should do that part of the work which we advise, at those times and places which we judge most for His glory.

¶ 114. Smaller advices which might be of use to us, are perhaps these: 1. Be sure never to disappoint a congregation. 2. Begin at the time appointed. 3. Let your whole deportment be serious, weighty, and solemn. 4. Always suit your subject to your audience. 5. Choose the plainest text you can. 6. Take care not to ramble, but keep to your text, and make out what you take in hand. 7. Take care of any thing awkward or affected, either in your gesture, phrase, or pronunciation. 8. Do not usually pray *extempore* above eight or ten minutes (at most) without intermission. 9. Frequently read and enlarge upon a portion of Scripture; and let young preachers often exhort without taking a text. 10. Always avail yourself of the great festivals by preaching on the occasion.

The Duty of Preachers to God, Themselves, and One Another.

¶ 115. The duty of a Preacher is,— 1. To preach. 2. To meet the societies and classes. 3. To visit the sick.

¶ 116. A Preacher shall be qualified for his charge by walking closely with God, and having his work greatly at heart, and by understanding and loving discipline, ours in particular.

¶ 117. We do not sufficiently watch over each other. Should we not frequently ask each other, Do you walk closely with God? Have you now fellowship with the Father and the Son? At what hour do you rise? Do you punctually observe the morning and evening hours of retirement? Do you spend the day in the manner in which the Conference advises? Do you converse seriously, usefully, and closely? To be more particular: Do you use all the means of grace yourself, and enforce the use of them on all other persons?

¶ 118. The means of grace are either instituted or prudential.

¶ 119. The INSTITUTED are:—

§ 1. *Prayer:* private, family, and public; consisting of deprecation, petition, intercession, and thanksgiving. Do you use each of these? Do you forecast daily, wherever you are, to secure time for private devotion? Do you practice it every-where? Do you ask every-where, Have you family prayer? Do you ask individuals, Do you use private prayer every morning and evening in particular?

§ 2. *Searching the Scriptures*, by 1. Reading: constantly, some part of every day; regularly, all the Bible in order; carefully, with notes; seriously, with prayer before and after; fruitfully, immediately practicing what you learn there. 2. Meditating: At set times. By rule. 3. Hearing: Every opportunity. With prayer before, at, after. Have you a Bible always about you?

§ 3. *The Lord's Supper:* Do you use this at every opportunity? With solemn prayer before? With earnest and deliberate self-devotion?

§ 4. *Fasting:* Do you use as much abstinence and fasting every week as your health, strength, and labor will permit?

§ 5. *Christian conference:* Are you convinced how important and how difficult it is to order your conversation aright? Is it always in grace? Seasoned with salt? Meet to minister grace to the hearers? Do you not converse too long at a time? Is not an hour commonly enough? Would it not be well always to have a determined end in view? And to pray before and after it?

¶ **120.** PRUDENTIAL means we may use either as Christians, as Methodists, or as Preachers.

§ 1. *As Christians:* What particular rules have you in order to grow in grace? What arts of holy living?

§ 2. *As Methodists:* Do you never miss your class?

§ 3. *As Preachers:* Have you thoroughly considered your duty? And do you make a conscience of executing every part of it? Do you meet every Society and their Leaders?

¶ 121. These means may be used without fruit. But there are some means which cannot: namely, watching, denying ourselves, taking up our cross, exercise of the presence of God.

§ 1. Do you steadily watch against the world? Yourself? Your besetting sin?

§ 2. Do you deny yourself every useless pleasure of sense? Imagination? Honor? Are you temperate in all things? For instance, in food, 1. Do you use only that kind and that degree which is best both for body and soul? Do you see the necessity of this? Do you eat no more at each meal than is necessary? Are you not heavy or drowsy after dinner? 3. Do you use only that kind, and that degree of drink, which is best both for your body and soul? Do you choose and use water for your common drink? And only take wine medicinally or sacramentally?

§ 3. Wherein do you take up your cross daily? Do you cheerfully bear your cross, however grievous to nature, as a gift of God, and labor to profit thereby?

§ 4. Do you endeavor to set God always before you? To see his eye continually fixed upon you?

¶ **122.** Never can you use these means but a blessing will ensue. And the more you use them, the more you will grow in grace.

The Necessity of Union among Ourselves.

¶ **123.** Let us be deeply sensible (from what we have known) of the evil of a division in principle, spirit, or practice, and the dreadful consequences to ourselves and others. If we are united, what can stand before us? If we divide, we shall destroy ourselves, the work of God, and the souls of our people.

¶ **124.** In order to a closer union with each other—1. Let us be deeply convinced of the absolute necessity of it. 2. Pray earnestly for, and speak freely to, each other. 3. When we meet, let us never part without prayer. 4. Take great care not to despise each other's gifts. 5. Never speak lightly of each other. 6. Let us defend each other's character in every thing so far as is consistent with truth. 7. Labor in honor each to prefer the other before himself. 8. We recommend a serious perusal of *The Causes, Evils, and Cures of Heart and Church Divisions.*

How we can Employ our Time Profitably when not Traveling, or engaged in Public Exercises.

¶ 125. As a general method of employing our time, we advise you,—1. As often as possible to rise at four. 2. From four to five in the morning, and from five to six in the evening, to meditate, pray, and read the Scriptures with notes, and the closely practical parts of what Mr. Wesley has published. 3. From six in the morning till twelve, wherever it is practicable, let the time be spent in appropriate reading, study, and private devotion.

¶ 126. Other reasons may concur, but the chief reason that the people under our care are not better is, because we are not more knowing and more holy.

¶ 127. And we are not more knowing, because we are idle. We forget our first rule: "Be diligent. Never be unemployed. Never be triflingly employed.

Neither spend any more time at any place than is strictly necessary." We fear there is altogether a fault in this matter, and that few of us are clear. Which of us spend as many hours a day in God's work as we did formerly in man's work? We talk—talk—or read what comes next to hand. We must, absolutely must, cure this evil, or betray the cause of God? But how? 1. Read the most useful books, and that regularly and constantly. 2. Steadily spend all the morning in this employment, or at least five hours in the four and twenty. "But I have no taste for reading." Contract a taste for it by use, or return to your former employment. "But I have no books." Be diligent to spread the books, and you will have the use of them.

Of our Deportment at the Conferences.

¶ 128. It is desired that all things be considered on these occasions as in the immediate presence of God; that every person speak freely whatever is in his heart.

¶ 129. In order, therefore, that we may best improve our time at the Conferences,

1. While we are conversing let us have an especial care to set God always before us. 2. In the intermediate hours, let us redeem all the time we can for private exercises. 3. Therein let us give ourselves to prayer for one another, and for a blessing on our labor.

The Matter and Manner of Preaching.

¶ 130. The best general method of preaching is, 1. To convince; 2. To offer Christ; 3. To invite; 4. To build up: And to do this in some measure in every sermon.

¶ 131. The most effectual way of preaching Christ is, to preach him in all his offices; and to declare his law, as well as his Gospel, both to believers and unbelievers. Let us strongly and closely insist upon inward and outward holiness in all its branches.

Rules by which we should continue, or desist from, Preaching at any Place.

¶ 132. It is by no means advisable for us to preach in as many places as we can without forming any societies. We have made the trial in various places, and that for a considerable time. But all the seed has fallen by the way-side There is scarcely any fruit remaining.

¶ **133.** We should endeavor to preach most, 1. Where there is the greatest number of quiet and willing hearers. 2. Where there is most fruit.

¶ **134.** We ought diligently to observe in what places God is pleased at any time to pour out his Spirit more abundantly, and at that time to send more laborers than usual into that part of the harvest.

Visiting from House to House, guarding against those Things that are so common to Professors, and enforcing Practical Religion.

¶ **135.** We can further assist those under our care by instructing them at their own houses. What unspeakable need is there of this! The world says, "*The Methodists are no better than other people.*" This is not true in the general; but,—

§ 1. Personal religion, either toward God or man, is too superficial among us. We can but just touch on a few particulars. How little faith is there among us! How little communion with God! How little living in heaven, walking in eternity, deadness to every creature! How much love of the world! Desire of pleasure, of ease, of getting money! How little brotherly love! What continual judging one another! What gossiping, evil-speaking, tale-bearing! What want of moral honesty! To instance only one particular: Who does as he would be done by in buying and selling.

§ 2. Family religion is wanting in many branches. And what avails public preaching alone, though we could preach like angels? We must, yea, every Traveling Preacher must, instruct the people from house to house. Till this be done, and that in good earnest, Methodists will be no better.

§ 3. Our religion is not sufficiently deep, universal, uniform; but superficial, partial, uneven. It will be so till we spend half as much time in this visiting as we now do in talking uselessly. Can we find a better method of doing this than Mr. Baxter's? If not, let us adopt it without delay. His whole tract, entitled "*Gildas Salvianus;* or, The Reformed Pastor," is well worth a careful perusal. Speaking of this visiting from house to house, he says, (p. 351,) "We shall find many hinderances, both in ourselves and the people." 1. In ourselves there is much dullness and laziness, so that there will be much ado to get us to be faithful in the work. 2. We have a base, man-pleasing temper, so that we let people perish rather than lose their love; we let them go quietly to hell lest we should offend them. 3. Some of us have also a foolish bashfulness. We know not how to begin, and blush to contradict the devil. 4. But the greatest hinderance is weakness of faith. Our whole motion is weak, because the spring of it is weak. 5. Lastly, we are unskillful in the work. How few know how to deal with men, so as to get within them, and suit all our discourse to their several conditions and tempers; to choose the fittest subjects and follow them with a holy mixture of seriousness, terror, love, and meekness!

¶ **136.** But undoubtedly this private application is implied in those solemn words of the apostle: "I charge thee before God and the Lord Jesus Christ, who shall judge the quick and the dead at his appearing, preach the word; be instant in season, out of season; reprove, rebuke, exhort, with all long-suffering."

¶ **137.** O brethren, if we could but set this work on foot in all our Societies, and prosecute it zealously, what glory would redound to God! If the common lukewarmness were banished, and every shop, and every house, busied in speaking of the word and works of God, surely God would dwell in our habitations, and make us his delight.

¶ **138.** And this is absolutely necessary to the welfare of our people, some of whom neither repent nor believe to this day. Look around, and see how many of them are still in apparent danger of damnation. And how can you walk, and talk, and be merry with such people, when you know their case? When you look them in the face, you should break forth into tears, as the prophet did when he looked upon Hazael, and then set on them with the most vehement exhortations. O, for God's sake, and the sake of poor souls, bestir yourselves, and spare no pains that may conduce to their salvation! What cause have we to bleed before the Lord that we have so long neglected this good work! If we had but engaged in it sooner, how many more might have been brought to Christ! And how much holier and happier might our Societies have been before now! And why might we not have done it sooner? There were many hinderances; and so there always will be. But the greatest hinderance is in ourselves, in our littleness of faith and love.

¶ **139.** But it is objected:—

§ 1. "This will take up so much time that we shall not have leisure to follow our studies." We answer, 1. Gaining knowledge is a good thing, but saving souls is a better. 2. By this very thing you will gain the most excellent knowledge, that of God and eternity. 3. You will have time for gaining other knowledge too. Only sleep no more than you need; "and never be idle, or triflingly employed." But, 4. If you can do but one, let your studies alone. We ought to throw by all the libraries in the world, rather than be guilty of the loss of one soul.

§ 2. "The people will not submit to it." If some will not, others will. And the success with them will repay all your labor. O let us herein follow the example of St. Paul! 1. For our general business, *Serving the Lord with all humility of mind:* 2. Our special work, *Take heed to yourselves and to all the flock:* 3. Our doctrine, *Repentance toward God, and faith toward our Lord Jesus Christ:* 4. The place, *I have taught you publicly, and from house to house:* 5. The object and manner of teaching, *I ceased not to warn every one night and day, with tears:* 6. His innocence and self-denial herein, *I have coveted no man's silver or gold:* 7. His patience, *Neither count I my life dear unto myself.* And among all other motives let these be ever before our eyes: (1) *The Church of God, which he hath purchased with his own blood:* (2) *Grievous wolves shall enter in; yea, of yourselves shall men arise, speaking perverse things.*

¶ **140.** Write this upon your hearts, and it will do you more good than twenty years' study. Then you will have no time to spare: you will have work enough. Then likewise no preacher will stay with us who is as salt that has lost its savor. For to such this employment would be mere drudgery. And in order to it, you will have need of all the knowledge you can procure, and grace you can attain.

¶ **141.** The sum is, Go into every house in course, and teach every one therein, young and old, to be Christians inwardly and outwardly; make every particular plain to their understandings; fix it in their minds; write it on their hearts. In order to this, there must be precept upon precept, line upon line. What patience, what love, what knowledge is requisite for this! We must needs do this, were it only to avoid idleness. Do we not loiter away many hours in every week? Each try himself; no idleness is consistent with a growth in grace. Nay without exactness in redeeming time, you cannot retain the grace you receive in justification.

¶ **142.** Why are we not more holy? why do we not live in eternity? walk with God all the day long? why are we not all devoted to God? breathing the whole spirit of missionaries? Chiefly because we are enthusiasts; looking for the end without using the means. To touch only upon two or three instances: Who of us rise at four or even at five, when we do not preach? Do we know the obligation and benefit of fasting or abstinence? How often do we practice it? The neglect of this alone is sufficient to account for our feebleness and faintness of spirit. We are continually grieving the Holy Spirit of God by the habitual neglect of a plain duty. Let us amend from this hour.

¶ 143. In order to guard against Sabbath-breaking, evil speaking, unprofitable conversation, lightness, expensiveness or gayety of apparel, and contracting debts without due care to discharge them,—1. Let us preach expressly on each of these heads. 2. Read in every Society the sermon on evil-speaking. 3. Let the Leaders closely examine and exhort every person to put away the accursed thing. 4. Let the Preachers warn every Society that none who is guilty herein can remain with us. 5. Extirpate out of our Church buying or selling goods which have not paid the duty laid upon them by government. Let none remain with us who will not totally abstain from this evil in every kind and degree. Extirpate bribery—receiving any thing, directly or indirectly—for voting at any election. Show no respect to persons herein, but expel all that touch the accursed thing. And strongly advise our people to discountenance all treats given by candidates before or at elections, and not to be partakers, in any respect, of such iniquitous practices.

Method of Receiving Traveling Preachers on Trial.

¶ **144.** A Preacher is to be received on trial,—1. By the Annual Conference. 2. In the interval of the Conference by a Bishop or the Presiding Elder of the District, until the sitting of the Conference.

¶ **145.** But no one should be received unless he first procure a recommendation from the Quarterly Conference of his Circuit or Station. We may then, if he give us satisfaction, receive him on trial. But before any such candidate is received on trial, or into full connection, or is ordained Deacon or Elder, he shall give satisfactory evidence respecting his knowledge of those particular subjects which have been recommended to his consideration.

¶ **146.** When a Preacher's name is not printed in the Minutes, he must receive a written license from a Bishop or Presiding Elder; but while he is on trial, the Annual Conference alone has jurisdiction over the question of his authority to preach: and his continuance on trial shall be equivalent to the renewal of his license to preach.

¶ 147. Observe! taking on trial is entirely different from admitting a preacher into full connection. One on trial may be either admitted or rejected without doing him any wrong: otherwise it would be no trial at all.

¶ 148. At each Annual Conference, those who are received on trial, or are admitted into full connection, shall be asked whether they are willing to devote themselves to the missionary work, and a list of the names of all those who are willing to do so shall be taken and reported to the Corresponding Secretaries of the Missionary Society; and all such shall be considered as ready and willing to be employed as missionaries whenever called for by either of the Bishops.

Manner of Receiving Traveling Preachers into Full Connection.

¶ 149. In receiving a Preacher at the Conference into full connection, after solemn fasting and prayer, every person proposed shall be asked, before the Conference, the following questions, (with any others which may be thought necessary,) namely:—

1. Have you faith in Christ?
2. Are you going on to perfection?
3. Do you expect to be made perfect in love in this life?
4. Are you groaning after it?
5. Are you resolved to devote yourself wholly to God and his work?
6. Do you know the rules of Society?
7. Do you keep them?
8. Do you constantly attend the sacrament?
9. Have you read the Form of Discipline?
10. Are you willing to conform to it?
11. Have you considered the rules of a Preacher, especially the first, tenth, and twelfth?
12. Will you keep them for conscience' sake?
13. Are you determined to employ all your time in the work of God?
14. Will you endeavor not to speak too long or too loud?
15. Will you diligently instruct the children in every place?

16. Will you visit from house to house?

17. Will you recommend fasting or abstinence, both by precept and example?

18. Are you in debt?

¶ **150.** Then if he give us satisfaction, after he has been employed two successive years in the regular itinerant work on Circuit, in Stations, or in our institutions of learning, which is to commence from his being received on trial at the Annual Conference, and being approved by the Annual Conference, and examined by the President of the Conference, he may be received into full connection.

¶ **151.** A Missionary employed on a Foreign Mission may be admitted into full connection, if recommended by the Superintendent of the Mission where he labors, without being present at the Annual Conference for examination.

The Reception of Ministers from other Evangelical Churches.

¶ **152.** Ministers who may offer to unite with us from other Christian Churches shall be received in the following manner:

§ 1. If they come to us properly accredited from any branch of the Methodist Church, or from any Church agreeing with us in doctrine, they may be received either as Local or Itinerant Ministers, according to such credentials, by giving satisfaction to an Annual or Quarterly Conference of their literary qualifications, and of their willingness to conform to our Church government and usages.

§ 2. Those ministers of other evangelical Churches who may desire to unite with our Church may be received according to our usages as Deacons or Elders, on condition of their taking upon them our ordination vows, without re-imposition of hands, if they shall give satisfaction to an Annual Conference of their being in orders, and of their agreement with us in doctrines, in discipline, and usages; *provided*, the Conference is also satisfied with their literary qualifications, gifts, grace, and usefulness.

¶ **153.** Whenever a minister is received according to either of the foregoing sections, he shall be furnished with a certificate, signed by a Bishop or a Presiding Elder, in the following words, namely: "This is to certify that ——— has been admitted into ——— Conference as a

Traveling Preacher, [or has been admitted as a Local Preacher on ——— Circuit,] he having been ordained to the office of a Deacon, [or an Elder, as the case may be,] according to the usages of the ——— Church, of which he has been a member and minister; and he is hereby authorized to exercise the functions pertaining to his office in the Methodist Episcopal Church so long as his life and conversation are such as become the Gospel of Christ.

"Given under my hand and seal, at ———, this ——— day of ———, in the year of our Lord ———. ———."

¶ 154. Preachers of other denominations who are not in orders may be received as Licentiates, provided they give satisfaction to a Quarterly or an Annual Conference that they are suitable persons to exercise the office, and of their agreement with the doctrines, discipline, government, and usages of our Church.

The Election of Bishops, and their Duty.

¶ 155. A Bishop is to be constituted by the election of the General Conference, and the laying on of the hands of three Bishops, or at least of one Bishop and two Elders. But the General Conference may authorize the election of a Missionary Bishop in the interim of the General Conference.

¶ 156. If by death, or otherwise, there be no Bishop remaining in our Church, the General Conference shall elect a Bishop, and the Elders, or any three of them, who shall be appointed by the General Conference for that purpose, shall consecrate him according to the Ritual.

¶ 157. The duties of a Bishop are,—

§ 1. To preside in our Conferences.

§ 2. To form the Districts according to his judgment.

§ 3. To fix the appointments of the Preachers; provided he shall not allow any Preacher to remain in the same Station more than three years successively; except the Presiding Elders; the Corresponding Secretaries of the Missionary Society; the Corresponding Secretary and Assistant Corresponding Secretaries of the

Board of Church Extension; the Corresponding Secretary of the Freedmen's Aid Society; the Editors, Assistant Editors, and Agents at New York and Cincinnati; the Editors and Assistant Editors at Syracuse, Pittsburgh, Chicago, St. Louis, Portland, San Francisco, Atlanta, and New Orleans; the Editor of the Zion's Herald; missionaries among the Indians, Welsh, Swedes, Norwegians, and other missionaries among foreigners, (not including the Germans,) where supplies are difficult to be obtained; missionaries to neglected portions of our cities, and to our people of color and on foreign stations; chaplains to reformatory, sanitary, and charitable institutions, to prisons, and in the army and navy; those Preachers who may be appointed to labor for the special benefit of seamen, and for the American Bible Society, or for any State Bible Society auxiliary thereto; the presidents, principals, or teachers of Seminaries of learning, which are or may be under our superintendence; or the Preacher stationed at Five Points Mission in New York, or at the American Chapel in Paris; and also when requested by an Annual Conference, to appoint a Preacher for a longer time than three years to any seminary of learning not under our care: *provided*, also, that, with the exceptions above named, he shall not continue a Preacher in the same appointment more than three years in six. He shall have authority, when requested by an Annual Conference, to appoint an agent, whose duty it shall be to travel throughout the bounds of such Conference, for the purpose of distributing tracts; an agent to promote the cause of temperance; and also to appoint an agent or agents for the benefit of our literary institutions; an agent for the German publishing fund; and for other benevolent institutions.

§ 4. In the intervals of the Conferences, to change, receive, and suspend Preachers as necessity may require, and as the Discipline directs.

§ 5. To travel through the Connection at large.

§ 6. To oversee the spiritual and temporal business of our Church.

§ 7. To consecrate Bishops, and ordain Elders and Deacons.

§ 8. To decide all questions of law involved in proceedings pending in an Annual Conference, subject to an appeal to the General Conference; but in all cases the application of law shall be with the Conference.

§ 9. To prescribe a course of study in English literature and in science, upon which those applying for admission upon trial in the Annual Conferences shall be examined and approved before such admission; and also to prescribe a course of reading and study proper to be pursued by candidates for the ministry for the term of four years.

¶ 158. A Bishop may, when he judges it necessary, unite two or more Circuits or Stations for Quarterly Conference purposes, without affecting their separate financial interests or pastoral duties.

¶ 159. If a Bishop cease from traveling at large among the people without the consent of the General Conference, he shall not thereafter exercise, in any degree, the Episcopal office in our Church.

¶ 160. In case there be no Bishop to travel at large through the Districts and exercise the Episcopal office, on account of death or otherwise, the Districts shall be regulated in every respect by the Annual Conferences and the Presiding

Elders in the interval of General Conference, ordination excepted.

Presiding Elders and their Duty.

¶ 161. Presiding Elders are to be chosen by the Bishops, by whom they are also to be stationed and changed.

¶ 162. A Bishop may allow an Elder to preside in the same District for any term not exceeding four years; after which he shall not be appointed to the same District for six years; but Presiding Elders in Missions and Mission Conferences in heathen lands may be appointed to the same District for more than four successive years.

¶ 163. The duties of a Presiding Elder are,—

§ 1. To travel through his appointed District.

§ 2. In the absence of the Bishop, to take charge of all the Elders and Deacons, Traveling and Local Preachers and Exhorters, in his District.

§ 3. To change, receive, and suspend Preachers in his District during the intervals of the Conferences, and in the absence of the Bishop, as the Discipline directs; *provided*, however, that a Presiding Elder shall not change a Preacher in his District from a charge to which he has been appointed by the Bishop, and appoint him to another to which he could not be legally appointed by the Bishop. The law of limitation applies also to Superannuated and Local Preachers who are employed in the pastoral work.

§ 4. To be present at, as far as practicable, and to hold, all the quarterly meetings, especially the first and fourth, and to call together the Quarterly Conference to hear complaints, to receive and try appeals, to renew all licenses approved by the Quarterly Conference, and to transact such other business as is provided for in the section on "The Quarterly Conferences," and to furnish the member of the General Missionary Committee for his Mission District a written statement of the condition of the missions under his care, and their pecuniary wants, prior to the annual meeting of the Committee.

§ 5. To oversee the spiritual and temporal business of the Church in his District, and to promote by all proper means the cause of Missions, Church Extension, and Sunday-schools; and to report to the Annual Conference the statistics of the Literary and Theological Institutions located within the bounds of his District, and under the care of our Church, according to the form published in the Appendix of the Discipline; and carefully to inquire at each Quarterly Conference whether the Rules respecting the Instruction of Children have been faithfully observed; and to report to the Annual Conference the names of all Traveling Preachers within his District who shall neglect to observe these Rules.

§ 6. To take care that every part of our Discipline be enforced in his District; to decide all questions of law involved in proceedings pending in a District or Quarterly Conference, subject to an appeal to the President of the next Annual Conference; but in all cases the application of law shall be with the Conference.

§ 7. To attend the Bishop when present in his District; and to give him, when absent, all necessary information, by letter, of the state of his District.

§ 8. To direct the candidates for the ministry who are admitted on trial to those studies which have been recommended by the Bishops.

§ 9. To explain to those Preachers who are on trial, as well as to those who are in future to be proposed for trial, that they may be either admitted or rejected without doing them any wrong.

¶ 164. If any Preacher absent himself from his Circuit, the Presiding Elder shall, as far as possible, fill his place with another Preacher, who shall be paid for his labors out of the allowance of the absent Preacher, in proportion to his usual allowance.

¶ 165. A Presiding Elder shall not have power to employ a Preacher who has been rejected by the previous Annual Conference, unless the Conference should give him liberty, under certain conditions.

The Election of Traveling Elders, and their Duty.

¶ 166. An Elder is constituted by the election of a majority of the Annual Con ference, and by the laying on of the hands of a Bishop and some of the Elders who are present.

¶ **167.** The duty of a Traveling Elder is—1. To administer Baptism and the Lord's Supper, to solemnize Matrimony, and to conduct divine worship. 2. To do all the duties of a Traveling Preacher.

¶ **168.** No Elder who ceases to travel, without the consent of the Annual Conference, certified under the hand of the President of the Conference, except in case of sickness, debility, or other unavoidable circumstance, shall on any account exercise the peculiar functions of his office, or even be allowed to preach among us: *nevertheless*, the final determination in all such cases is with the Annual Conference.

¶ **169.** Every Traveling Deacon shall exercise his office for two years, before he be eligible to the office of Elder; except in the case of missions, when the Annual Conferences shall have authority to elect for the Elder's office sooner, if they judge it expedient.

¶ **170.** When a Preacher shall have passed his examination, and been admitted into Full Connection, and elected to the office of a Deacon, but fails of his ordination through the absence of the Bishop, his eligibility to the office of

Elder shall run from the time of his election to the office of a Deacon.

The Election of Traveling Deacons and their Duty.

¶ **171.** A Traveling Deacon is constituted by the election of a majority of the Annual Conference, and the laying on of the hands of a Bishop.

¶ **172.** The duty of a Traveling Deacon is—1. To administer Baptism and to solemnize Matrimony. 2. To assist the Elder in administering the Lord's Supper. 3. To do all the duties of a Traveling Preacher.

¶ **173.** Whenever a Preacher on Trial shall be appointed by a Bishop to a mission, or a chaplaincy in the army or navy, or in reformatory, sanitary, or charitable institutions, or prisons, he may, if elected by an Annual Conference, with the approbation of a Bishop, be ordained by him before his probation ends.

¶ **174.** No Deacon who ceases to travel without the consent of the Annual Conference, certified under the hand of the President of the Conference, except in cases of sickness, debility, or other unavoidable circumstances, shall on any account exercise the peculiar functions of his office, or even be allowed to preach, among us: *nevertheless*, the final determination in all such cases is with the Annual Conference.

The Duties of those who have the Charge of Circuits or Stations.

¶ 175. The duties of the Elder, Deacon, or Preacher who has the special charge of a Circuit, are,—

§ 1. To have the oversight of the other Preachers in his Circuit or Station.

§ 2. To renew the tickets for the admission of members into Love-feasts quarterly.

§ 3. To appoint all the Leaders, to change them when he sees it necessary, and to examine each of them, with all possible exactness, at least once a quarter, concerning his method of meeting a class.

§ 4. To receive, try, and expel members, according to the Form of Discipline.

§ 5. To hold Watch-nights and Love-feasts.

§ 6. To hold Quarterly Meetings in the absence of the Presiding Elder.

§ 7. To take care that every Society be duly supplied with books.

§ 8. To hold a meeting of all the Leaders and Stewards of the Charge, to be denominated the Leaders and Stewards' Meeting, as often as practicable, in order to inquire, 1. Are there any sick? 2. Are there any requiring temporal relief? 3. Are there any who walk disorderly and will not be reproved? 4. Are there any who willfully neglect the means of grace? 5. Are any changes to be made in the classes? 6. Are there any probationers to be recommended for reception into full connection? 7. Are there any to be recommended for license to exhort or to preach? 8. What amount has been received for the support of the Pastor or Pastors? 9. Is there any miscellaneous business?

§ 9. To catechise the children publicly in the Sunday-school and at special meetings appointed for that purpose. It shall also be the duty of each Preacher, in his report to each Quarterly Conference, to state to what extent he has publicly or privately catechised the children of his Charge.

§ 10. To form classes for the instruction of the larger children, youth, and adults in the word of God, and to attend to all the duties prescribed for the training of children.

§ 11. To give an account of his Circuit every quarter to his Presiding Elder.

§ 12. To make a written report at each Quarterly Conference, as follows, namely:—

QUARTERLY REPORT

Of the Preacher in Charge of ——— to the ——— Quarterly Conference, held at———, ———, 18—.

Number of Sunday-schools within the bounds of the Charge..................
State of Sunday-schools within the bounds of the Charge........................
Average attendance......................
Number of scholars fifteen years of age and over....................................
Average attendance......................

I have preached —— times to the children, and catechised them —— times during the quarter.

Classes of Children formed for Religious Instruction..........................
Received into Full Membership...........
Excluded from the Church ....
Received by Letter.........................
Dismissed by Letter.........................
Deceased during the Quarter..............
Withdrawn from the Church...............

The following Pastoral labor has been bestowed:—

....

Benevolent Collections during the —— quarter, as follows:—
Missionary..............................
Church Extension........................
Tract...................................
Sunday-school...........................
Other objects, namely...................

The following is to be used only at the fourth Quarterly Conference:—

Subscribers have been obtained for our periodicals as follows:—
——— Advocate........................
Ladies' Repository......................
Quarterly Review........................
Sunday-school Advocate..................
Sunday-school Teachers' Journal.........
Missionary Advocate.....................

Respectfully submitted,
——————, *Preacher in Charge.*

§ 13. To report the names at each Love-feast of those who have been received into the Church, or excluded therefrom, during the quarter; also the names of those who have been received or dismissed by certificate, and of those who have died or have withdrawn from the Church.

§ 14. To lay before the Quarterly Conference, at each quarterly meeting, to be entered on its journal, a written statement of the number, state, and average attendance of the Sunday-schools in the Circuit or Station, and to report the same to the Annual Conference according to the form published by the Sunday-school Union of the Methodist Episcopal Church, together with the amount raised for the support of Missions, and for the publication of Tracts.

§ 15. To take an exact account of all the matters specified in ¶ 77, and report them to the Annual Conference, that their number may be printed in the Minutes, and also to register the Marriages and Baptisms.

§ 16. To examine the accounts of all the Stewards.

§ 17. To appoint a person to receive the quarterly collection in the *classes.*

§ 18. To see that *public* collections be made quarterly, if need be.

§ 19. To encourage the support of Missions, Church Extension, and Sunday-schools, and the publication and distribution of Bibles, tracts, and Sunday-school books, by forming societies and making collections for these objects in such way and manner as the Annual Conference to which he belongs shall from time to time direct. If the Annual Conference to which he belongs should not give any directions on the subject, to take up a collection in the course of the year, or raise a subscription, as he may judge expedient, the proceeds of which shall be at his disposal for the purchase and distribution of tracts.

§ 20. To take an annual collection in each of his appointments in behalf of the Sunday-school Union.

§ 21. To take a collection annually in each of his appointments in behalf of the Board of Church Extension.

§ 22. To defray the expenses of the Delegates composing the General Conference, a collection shall be taken up in each Circuit and Station some time previous to the sitting of the Conference, and the sums so collected shall be brought up by the delegation to the General Conference, and applied to the object herein contemplated, in proportion to the expenses of the several Delegates.

¶ **176.** It shall be the further duty of the Preacher in Charge:—

§ 1. To make a regular catalogue of

the Societies in towns and cities, as they live in the streets.

§ 2. To leave his successor a particular account of the Circuit, including an account of the subscribers for our periodicals.

§ 3. To enforce vigorously, but calmly, the rules of the Society.

§ 4. To suffer no Love-feast to last above an hour and a half.

§ 5. To warn all from time to time that none are to remove from one Circuit to another without a note of recommendation from the Preacher of the Circuit in these words: "*A. B., the bearer, has been an acceptable member of the Methodist Episcopal Church.*" And to inform them that, without such a certificate, they will not be received into the Church in other places. And also to notify of such certificate and removal the Pastors of those charges within the bounds of which persons having received such certificates shall have removed: *provided*, that, when a member wishes to remove his residence out of any particular charge, and there are, in the judgment of the Preacher in Charge, sufficient reasons for withholding a certificate, and the member is willing to be tried, he shall be held guilty of maladministration unless he proceed in the trial of such person. A Preacher may give a note of recommendation to any member who wishes to unite with any other evangelical denomination.

§ 6. To recommend every-where decency and cleanliness.

§ 7. To read the Rules of the Society, with the aid of the other Preachers, once a year in every congregation, and once a quarter in every Society.

§ 8. The Preacher who has the charge of a Circuit shall appoint prayer-meetings wherever he can in his Circuit.

§ 9. Wherever it is practicable he shall so arrange the appointments as to give the Local Preachers regular and systematic employment on the Sabbath.

§ 10. He shall take care that a fast be held in every Society in his Circuit on the Friday preceding every quarterly meeting, and that a memorandum of it be written on all the class papers.

§ 11. To license such persons as he may deem proper to officiate as Exhorters in the Church, according to the provisions of the Discipline.

¶ 177. In order to supply the Circuits during the sitting of the Conference:—

§ 1. Let all the appointments stand according to the plan of the Circuit.

§ 2. Engage as many Local Preachers and Exhorters as will supply them, and let them be paid for their time in proportion to the allowance of the Traveling Preachers.

§ 3. If Preachers and Exhorters cannot attend, let some person of ability be appointed in every Society to sing, pray, and read one of Mr. Wesley's sermons.

§ 4. But if that cannot be done let there be prayer-meetings.

¶ 178. The Preachers who have the oversight of Circuits are required to execute all our rules fully and strenuously against all frauds, and particularly against dishonest insolvencies, suffering none to remain in our Church on any account who are found guilty of any fraud.

Supernumerary and Superannuated Preachers.

¶ 179. A Supernumerary Preacher is one who, because of impaired health, is temporarily unable to perform effective work. He may receive an appointment, or be left without one, according to the judgment of the Annual Conference of which he is a member; but he shall have no claim on the beneficiary funds of the Church, except by vote of the Conference; and he shall be subject to all the limitations of the Discipline in respect to re-appointment and continuance in the same charge that apply to effective Preachers. In case he be left without an appointment he shall have a seat in the Quarterly Conference, and all the privileges of membership in the place where he may reside.

¶ **180.** Every Superannuated Preacher, who may reside without the bounds of the Conference of which he is a member, shall have a seat in the Quarterly Conference, and all the privileges of membership, in the Church where he may reside; and he shall annually forward to his Conference a certificate of his Christian and ministerial conduct, together with an account of the number and circumstances of his family, signed by the Presiding Elder of the District, or the Preacher in Charge of the Circuit or Station within whose bounds he may reside; without which the Conference shall not be required to allow his claim, and may locate him without his consent.

General Directions concerning Local Preachers.

¶ 181. The Quarterly Conference shall have authority to license proper persons to preach, and to renew their license annually, when, in the judgment of said Conference, their gifts, grace, and usefulness will warrant such renewal; to recommend to the Annual Conference Local Preachers who are suitable candidates for Deacons' or Elders' Orders, and for Admission on Trial in the traveling connection; and to try, suspend, and deprive of ministerial office and credentials, expel or acquit, any Local Preacher in the Circuit or Station against whom charges may be preferred; *provided*, That no person shall be licensed to preach without the recommendation of the Society of which he is a member, or of the Leaders and Stewards' Meeting; and no member of the Church shall be at liberty to preach without such license. Nor shall any one be licensed to preach, or recommended to the Annual Conference to travel, or for ordination, without first being examined in the District or Quarterly Conference on the subject of Doctrines and Discipline.

¶ 182. Every Local Elder, Deacon, or Preacher shall be amenable to the District or Quarterly Conference where he resides for his Christian character and the faithful performance of his ministerial office. He shall have his name recorded on the journal of said Conference, and also enrolled on a class paper, and shall meet in class; and in neglect of the above duties, or if found unacceptable in his ministerial office after due trial, the District or Quarterly Conference, if they judge it proper, may deprive him of his ministerial office. And when a Preacher is located, or discontinued by an Annual Conference, he shall be amenable to the Quarterly Conference of the Circuit or Station where he had his last appointment.

¶ 183. Whenever a Local Elder, Deacon, or Preacher shall remove from one Circuit or Station to another, he shall procure from the Presiding Elder of the

District, or from the Preacher having charge, a certificate of his official standing in the Church at the time of his removal, without which he shall not be received as a Local Preacher in other places.

¶ 184. The Presiding Elders and the Preachers in Charge are required so to arrange the appointments, wherever it is practicable, as to give the Local Preachers regular and systematic employment on the Sabbath.

¶ 185. Whenever a Local Preacher shall have a pastoral charge, he shall hold his Church relation in said Charge.

Local Preachers and their Ordination.

¶ 186. A licensed Local Preacher shall be eligible to the office of a Deacon after he has preached four consecutive years from the time he received a regular license, and has obtained a testimonial from the District or Quarterly Conference, after proper examination, signed by the President and countersigned by the Secretary, and after his character has passed in examination before, and he has obtained the approbation of, the Annual Conference.

¶ 187. A Local Preacher who has been licensed three consecutive years before his admission on trial in an Annual Conference shall be eligible to the office of Deacon after he has preached one year in the traveling connection, and has obtained a recommendation from the District or Quarterly Conference of which he is a member, and his character and qualifications have been examined and approved by the Annual Conference.

¶ 188. A Local Deacon shall be eligible to the office of an Elder after he has preached four years from the time he was ordained a Deacon, and has obtained a recommendation from the District or Quarterly Conference of which he is a member, certifying his qualifications in doctrine, discipline, talents, and usefulness, signed by the President and countersigned by the Secretary. He shall, if he cannot attend, send to the Annual Conference such recommendation, and a note certifying his belief in the Doctrines and Discipline of our Church. The whole being examined by the Annual Conference, and approved, he may be ordained.

Exhorters.

¶ 189. An Exhorter shall be constituted by the recommendation of the class of which he is a member, or of the Leaders and Stewards' Meeting of the Circuit or Station, and a license signed by the Preacher in Charge.

¶ 190. The duties of Exhorters are to hold meetings for prayer and exhortation wherever opportunity is afforded, subject to the direction of the Preacher in Charge; to attend all the sessions of the District and Quarterly Conferences; to be subject to an annual examination of character in the District or Quarterly Conference, and a renewal of license annually by the Presiding Elder, or Preacher having the charge, if approved by the District or Quarterly Conference.

PART II. — CHAPTER III.

STEWARDS.

Qualifications, Appointment, and Duties of Stewards.

¶ **191.** Let the Stewards be men of solid piety, who both know and love the Methodist doctrine and discipline, and of good natural and acquired abilities to transact the temporal business.

¶ **192.** In the appointment of the Stewards, the Preacher having the charge of the Circuit shall have the right of nomination; but the Quarterly Conference shall confirm or reject such nomination. The Stewards so appointed shall hold office for one year, but may be reappointed in like manner from year to year.

¶ **193.** The duties of Stewards are, to take an exact account of all the money or other provisions collected for the support of the Preachers in the Circuit or Station, and apply the same as the Discipline directs; to make an accurate return of every expenditure of money, whether to the Preachers, the sick, or the poor; to seek the needy and distressed in order to relieve and comfort them; to inform the Preachers of any sick or disorderly persons; to tell the Preachers what they think wrong in them; to attend the Quarterly Meetings of their Circuit, and the Leaders and Stewards' meetings; to give advice, if asked, in planning the Circuit; to attend committees for the application of money to Churches; to give counsel in matters of arbitration; to provide the elements for the Lord's Supper; to write circular letters to the Societies in the Circuit to be more liberal, if need be; as also to let them know, when occasion requires, the state of the temporal concerns at the last Quarterly Meeting.

¶ **194.** The duties of District Stewards are, to attend the annual District Stewards' Meeting when called by the Presiding Elder, and perform the duties specified in ¶ 348.

¶ **195.** Stewards are accountable for the faithful performance of their duty to the Quarterly Conference of the Circuit or Station, which shall have power to dismiss or change them at pleasure.

¶ **196.** There shall be not less than three nor more than nine Stewards in each Circuit or Station, one of whom shall be appointed Recording Steward by the Quarterly Conference after each annual election. But when two or more Circuits or Stations are united, the Stewards shall hold office till the first Quarterly Conference shall elect a new Board.

PART III.

ADMINISTRATION OF DISCIPLINE.

CHAPTER I.

BRINGING MINISTERS AND MEMBERS TO TRIAL, AND THE SETTLEMENT OF DISPUTES.

The Trial of a Bishop.

¶ 197. A Bishop is answerable for his conduct to the General Conference, which shall have power to order the manner of his trial.

¶ 198. When a Bishop is accused of immoral conduct, the Presiding Elder within whose District said immorality is alleged to have been committed shall call to his aid four Traveling Elders, which five ministers shall carefully inquire into the case; and if, in their judgment, there is reasonable ground for such accusation, they, or a majority of them, shall prepare and sign the proper charge in the case, and shall send a copy thereof, so signed, to the accused, and shall

9

give notice thereof to one of the Bishops. Said Bishop, so notified, shall convene a Judicial Conference, to be composed of the Triers of Appeals in the five neighboring Conferences. And the said Judicial Conference shall have full power to try the accused Bishop, and to suspend him from the functions of his office, or expel him from the Church, as they may deem his offense requires. One of the Bishops shall preside at his trial.

¶ 199. The accused shall have the right of peremptory challenge, yet not so as to reduce the number of the Judicial Conference below twenty-one.

¶ 200. When a Bishop is chargeable with imprudent conduct, a Presiding Elder shall take with him two Traveling Elders, and shall admonish the Bishop so offending. In case of a second offense, one of the Bishops, together with three Traveling Elders, shall call upon him and reprehend and admonish him. If he still persist in his imprudence, he shall then be tried in the manner ordered in ¶¶ 198, 199.

¶ 201. A Bishop shall have the right of appeal to the ensuing General Conference, if he signify his intention to appeal at the time of his conviction, or when informed thereof.

¶ **202.** Complaints against the administration of a Bishop may be forwarded to the General Conference, and entertained there: *provided* that, in its judgment, due notice has been given.

The Method of Proceeding against accused Traveling Ministers or Preachers.

¶ **203.** When an Elder, Deacon, or Preacher is under report of being guilty of some crime expressly forbidden in the word of God, sufficient to exclude a person from the kingdom of grace and glory,—

§ 1. In the interval of the Annual Conference let the Presiding Elder, in the absence of a Bishop, call as many Traveling Ministers as he shall think fit, at least five; and, if possible, bring the accused and the accuser face to face, and cause a correct record of the investigation to be kept and transmitted to the Annual Conference. If the person be clearly convicted, he shall be suspended from all ministerial services and Church privileges until the ensuing Annual Con ference, at which his case shall be fully considered and determined. But if the accused be a Presiding Elder, three of the Senior Preachers of his District shall inquire into the character of the report, and if they judge it necessary, call in the Presiding Elder of any adjoining District, who shall appoint a Committee of five Elders from within the bounds of the Annual Conference of which the accused is a member, and also preside at the examination.

§ 2. If the accused and accuser cannot be brought face to face, but the supposed delinquent flees from trial, it shall be received as a presumptive proof of guilt; and out of the mouth of two or three witnesses he shall be condemned: *nevertheless*, even in that case, the Annual Conference shall reconsider and determine the whole matter.

§ 3. And if the accused be a Superannuated or Supernumerary Preacher, living out of the bounds of the Conference of which he is a member, he shall be held responsible to the Annual Conference within whose bounds he may reside, who shall have power to try, acquit, suspend, locate, or expel him in the same manner as if he were a member of the said Conference.

¶ **204.** If the charge be preferred at the Conference, the case may be referred to a Committee, in the presence of a Presiding Elder or a member appointed by the Bishop in his stead, who shall cause a faithful record of the proceedings and testimony to be laid before the Conference; on which, with such other evidence as may be admitted, the case shall be decided.

¶ **205.** In cases of improper tempers, words, or actions, the person so offending shall be reprehended by his senior in office. Should a second transgression take place, one, two, or three Ministers or Preachers are to be taken as witnesses. If he be not then cured, let the Presiding Elder proceed as in ¶ 203, §§ 1, 2, 3.

¶ **206.** When a member of an Annual Conference fails in business, or contracts debts which he is not able to pay, let the Presiding Elder appoint three judicious members of the Church to inspect the accounts, contracts, and circumstances of the supposed delinquent, and if, in their opinion, he has behaved dishonestly, or contracted debts without the probability of paying, let the case be disposed of according to ¶ 203, §§ 1, 2, 3.

¶ **207.** When a Minister or Preacher holds and disseminates, publicly or privately, doctrines which are contrary to our Articles of Religion, let the same process be observed as in the case of gross immorality; but if the Minister or Preacher so offending do solemnly engage not to disseminate such erroneous doctrines, in public or in private, he shall be borne with till his case be laid before the next Annual Conference, which shall determine the matter.

¶ **208.** When a Traveling Minister is accused of being so unacceptable, inefficient, or secular, as to be no longer useful in his work, the Conference shall investigate the case, and if it appear that the complaint is well founded, and the accused will not voluntarily retire, the Conference may locate him without his consent.

¶ **209.** When a Traveling Preacher in the interim of an Annual Conference refuses to attend to the work assigned him, let the Presiding Elder proceed as directed in ¶ 203, §§ 1, 2, 3.

¶ **210.** A Preacher is answerable on a

complaint of maladministration to the Annual Conference of which he is a member.

¶ **211.** But should the Conference having jurisdiction in any of the foregoing cases judge it expedient to try the accused by a select number, it may appoint not less than nine nor more than fifteen of its members for that purpose, the accused having the right to challenge for cause, who, in the presence of a Bishop, or a chairman whom the President of the Conference shall appoint, and one or more of the Secretaries of the Conference, shall have full power to consider and determine the case according to the Rules which govern Annual Conferences in such proceedings; and they shall make a faithful report of all their doings to the Secretary of the Conference in writing, and deliver up to him the bill of charges, the evidence taken, and the decision rendered, with all other documents brought into the trial. Or the Annual Conference may, when a case cannot be tried during the session for want of testimony, refer it to the Presiding Elder having charge of the Preacher complained of, who shall proceed as directed in ¶ 203, §§ 1, 2, 3.

Proceedings against Preachers on Trial.

¶ 212. A Preacher on Trial who may be accused of crime shall be accountable to the Quarterly Conference of the Circuit on which he travels. The Presiding Elder shall call a Committee of three Local Preachers, which may suspend him; and the Quarterly Conference may expel him; *nevertheless*, he shall have a right to an appeal to the next Annual Conference.

The Trial of Local Preachers.

¶ 213. When a Local Elder, Deacon, or Preacher is reported to be guilty of some crime expressly forbidden in the word of God, sufficient to exclude a person from the kingdom of grace and glory, the Preacher having charge shall call a Committee, consisting of three or more Local Preachers, before which it shall be the duty of the accused to appear, and by which he shall be acquitted, or, if found guilty, suspended until the next District or Quarterly Conference. And the Preacher in Charge shall cause exact minutes of the charges, testimony, and examination, together with the decision of the Committee, to be laid before the District or Quarterly Conference, where it shall be the duty of the accused to appear. If the accused refuse or neglect to appear before said Committee, he may be tried in his absence.

¶ **214.** The President shall, at the commencement of the Trial, appoint a Secretary, who shall take down regular minutes of the evidence of the trial, which minutes, when read and approved, shall be signed by the President, and also by the members of the Conference who are present, or a majority of them.

¶ **215.** In case of improper tempers, words, or actions, the person so offending shall be reprehended by the Preacher having charge. Should a second transgression take place, one, two, or three friends are to be taken as witnesses. If he be not then cured he shall be tried at the next District or Quarterly Conference, and, if found guilty and impenitent, he shall be expelled from the Church.

¶ **216.** When a Local Elder, Deacon, or Preacher fails in business, or contracts debts which he is not able to pay, let the Preacher in Charge appoint three judicious members of the Church to inspect the accounts, contracts, and circumstances of the supposed delinquent; and if, in their opinion, he has behaved dishonestly, or contracted debts without the probability of paying, let the case be disposed of according to ¶ 213.

Trial of an Accused Member.

I. FOR IMMORAL CONDUCT.

¶ 217. An accused member shall be brought to trial before a Committee of not less than five, who shall not be members of the Quarterly Conference, (and, if the Preacher judge it necessary, he may select the Committee from any part of the District,) in the presence of the Preacher in charge, who shall preside in the trial, and cause exact minutes of the evidence and proceedings in the case to be taken. In the selection of the Committee, the parties may challenge for cause.

¶ 218. If the accused person be found guilty, by the decision of a majority of the Committee, and the crime be such as is expressly forbidden by the word of God, sufficient to exclude a person from the kingdom of grace and glory, let the Preacher in Charge expel him.

¶ **219.** If the accused person evade a trial, by absenting himself after sufficient notice given him, he may be tried in his absence, and if found guilty he shall be expelled.

II. NEGLECT OF THE MEANS OF GRACE.

¶ **220.** When members of our Church habitually neglect the means of grace, such as the public worship of God, the Supper of the Lord, family and private prayer, searching the Scriptures, class-meetings, and prayer-meetings,—1. Let the Elder, Deacon, or one of the Preachers, visit them whenever it is practicable, and explain to them the consequence if they continue to neglect. 2. If they do not amend, let him who has the charge of the Circuit or Station bring their case before the Society, or a select number, before whom they shall have been cited to appear; and if they be found guilty of willful neglect, by a decision of a majority of the members before whom their case is brought, let them be excluded.

III. IMPRUDENT CONDUCT.

¶ 221. But in cases of neglect of duties of any kind, imprudent conduct, indulging sinful tempers or words, the buying, selling, or using intoxicating liquors as a beverage, dancing, playing at games of chance, attending theaters, horse-races, circuses, dancing-parties, or patronizing dancing-schools, or taking such other amusements as are obviously of misleading or questionable moral tendency, or disobedience to the Order and Discipline of the Church; first, let private reproof be given by a Preacher or Leader, and if there be an acknowledgment of the fault, and proper humiliation, the person may be borne with. On a second offense, the Preacher or Leader may take one or two faithful friends. On a third offense, let him be brought to trial, and if found guilty, and there be no sign of real humiliation, he shall be expelled.

IV. FOR DISSENSION.

¶ 222. If a member of our Church shall be accused of endeavoring to sow dissension in any of our Societies, by inveighing against either our Doctrines or Discipline, the person so offending shall first be reproved by the Preacher in Charge, and if he persist in such pernicious practice he shall be brought to trial, and if found guilty, expelled.

V. DISAGREEMENT IN BUSINESS AND NON-PAYMENT OF DEBTS.

¶ **223.** On any disagreement between two or more members of our Church concerning business transactions, which cannot be settled by the parties, the Preacher in Charge shall inquire into the circumstances of the case, and shall recommend to the parties a reference, consisting of two arbiters chosen by the plaintiff and two chosen by the defendant, which four arbiters so chosen shall nominate a fifth; the five arbiters being members of our Church.

¶ **224.** If either party refuse to abide their judgment he shall be brought to trial, and if he fail to show sufficient cause for such refusal he shall be expelled.

¶ **225.** If any member of our Church shall refuse, in cases of debt or other disputes, to refer the matter to arbitration when recommended by the Preacher in

Charge, or shall enter into a lawsuit with another member before these measures are taken, he shall be brought to trial, and if he fail to show that the case is of such a nature as to require and justify a process at law he shall be expelled.

VI. INSOLVENCY ON THE PART OF ANY OF OUR MEMBERS.

¶ 226. The Preachers who have the oversight of Circuits and Stations are required to execute all our rules fully and strenuously against all frauds, and particularly against dishonest insolvencies, suffering none to remain in our Church on any account who are found guilty of any fraud.

¶ 227. To prevent scandal, when any of our members fail in business, or contract debts which they are not able to pay, let two or three judicious members of the Church inspect the accounts, contracts, and circumstances of the case of the supposed delinquent; and if they judge that he has behaved dishonestly, or borrowed money without a probability of paying, let him be brought to trial, and if found guilty, expelled.

VII. GENERAL DIRECTIONS.

¶ 228. In all the foregoing cases of trial, witnesses from without shall not be rejected; and the testimony of an absent witness may be taken before the Preacher in Charge, or a Preacher appointed by the Presiding Elder of the District within which such witness resides: *provided*, in every case sufficient notice has been given to the adverse party of the time and place of taking such testimony. The accused shall have the right to call to his assistance, as counsel, any member in good and regular standing in the Methodist Episcopal Church.

¶ 229. If in any of the above-mentioned cases the Preacher in Charge differ in judgment from the majority of the Committee concerning the guilt or innocence of the accused, he may refer the trial to the ensuing Quarterly Conference, which shall have authority to order a new trial.

¶ 230. When the Quarterly Conference, sitting as a Court of Appeals, remands a case for a new trial, the Preacher in Charge shall proceed to try the accused member again, unless the charges are withdrawn.

¶ **231.** After such forms of trial and expulsion, such persons shall have no privileges of Society or of Sacraments in our Church, without contrition, confession, and satisfactory reformation.

¶ **232.** In all cases of trial and appeal it is improper for the Presiding Officer to deliver a charge to the Committee explaining the evidence and setting forth the merits of the case.

PART III.—CHAPTER II.

TRIAL OF APPEALS.

Appeals of Traveling Ministers or Preachers.

¶ 233. In all cases of trial and conviction under the provisions of ¶¶ 203–211, an appeal shall be allowed to a Judicial Conference, constituted as hereinafter provided, if the condemned person signify his intention to appeal at the time of his conviction, or at any time thereafter when he is informed thereof.

¶ 234. The several Annual Conferences in the United States shall, at each session, select seven Elders, men of experience and of sound judgment in the affairs of the Church, who shall be known as Triers of Appeals.

¶ 235. When notice of appeal is given to the President of an Annual Conference, he shall proceed, with due regard to the wishes and rights of the appellant, to designate three Conferences, conveniently near that from which the appeal is taken, whose Triers of Appeals shall constitute a Judicial Conference, and to fix the time and place of its session, and to give notice thereof to all concerned.

¶ **236.** The appellant shall have the right of peremptory challenge, yet so that the Triers present, and ready to proceed with the hearing, shall not fall below thirteen, which number shall be required for a quorum.

¶ **237.** A Bishop shall preside in the Judicial Conference. The Conference shall appoint a Secretary, who shall keep a faithful record of all the proceedings, and shall, at the close of the trial, transmit the records made and the papers submitted in the case to the Secretary of the preceding General Conference, to be filed and preserved with the papers of that body.

¶ **238.** It shall be the duty of the Secretary of the Annual Conference carefully to preserve the minutes of the trial, whether before a Committee or before the Conference, and all the documents relating to the case, together with the charge or charges and the specification or specifications, which minutes and documents only, in case of an appeal from the decision of an Annual Conference, shall be presented to the Judicial Conference in evidence on the case.

¶ **239.** In all cases where an appeal is made, and admitted by the Judicial Conference, the appellant shall state, either personally or by his representative, (who shall be a member of an Annual Conference,) the grounds of his appeal, showing cause why he appeals, and he shall be allowed to make his appeal without interruption. After which the representatives of the Annual Conference from whose decision the appeal is made shall be permitted to respond in presence of the appellant, who shall have the privilege of replying to such representatives, which reply shall close the pleadings on both sides. This done, the parties shall withdraw, and the Judicial Conference shall decide the case.

¶ **240.** The General Conference shall carefully review the decisions of questions of law contained in the records and documents transmitted to it from the Judicial Conferences, and in case of serious error therein shall take such action as justice may require.

¶ **241.** Appeals from an Annual Conference in the United States not easily accessible may, at the discretion of the President thereof, be heard by a Judicial Conference selected from among the more central Conferences. Appeals from a Conference other than those in the United States may be heard by a Judicial Conference called to meet at or near New York by the Bishop in charge of said Conference; or the appeal may be heard directly by the General Conference.

¶ **242.** After a Preacher shall have been regularly tried and expelled he shall have no privileges of Society or Sacraments in our Church without confession, contrition, and satisfactory reformation.

Appeals of Local Preachers.

¶ **243.** In case of condemnation, the Local Preacher, Deacon, or Elder shall be allowed to appeal to the next Annual Conference, provided that he signify to the Quarterly Conference his determination to appeal; in which case the President shall lay the minutes of the trial before the said Annual Conference, at which the Local Preacher, Deacon, or

Elder, so appealing, may appear; and the said Annual Conference, by Committee, as in the case of accused Traveling Preachers, or in full session, shall judge, and finally determine from the minutes of the said trial so laid before them.

Appeals of Members.

¶ 244. If there be a murmur or complaint from any excluded person in any of the above-mentioned instances, (¶¶ 217–232,) that justice has not been done, he, not having absented himself from trial after due notice was given him, shall be allowed an appeal to the next Quarterly Conference; and no member thereof having been a member of the Committee for the trial of such person shall be permitted to vote on the case: and the Preacher in Charge shall present exact minutes of the evidence and proceedings of the trial to the Quarterly Conference, from which minutes the case shall finally be determined. And if, in the judgment of the Presiding Elder, because of local prejudice, an impartial trial cannot be had in the Quarterly Conference of the

Circuit or Station where the appellant resides, he may, on the demand of either party, cause the appeal to be tried by any other Quarterly Conference within his District, after due notice to the complainant and appellant.

PART III.—CHAPTER III.

RESTORATION OF CREDENTIALS OF ORDINATION.

Credentials of those who have been Traveling Preachers.

¶ 245. When any Traveling Elder or Deacon is deprived of his credentials, by expulsion or otherwise, they shall be filed with the papers of the Annual Conference of which he was a member; and should he, at any future time, give satisfactory evidence to the said Conference of his amendment, and procure a certificate of the Quarterly Conference of the Circuit or Station where he resides or of an Annual Conference who may have admitted him on trial, recommending to the Annual Conference of which he was formerly a member the restoration of his credentials, the said Conference may restore them.

Credentials of Local Preachers.

¶ **246.** When a Local Elder or Deacon shall be expelled, the Presiding Elder shall require of him the credentials of his ordination, to be filed with the papers of the Annual Conference within the limits of which the expulsion has taken place. And should he, at any future time, produce to the Annual Conference a certificate of his restoration, signed by the President and countersigned by the Secretary of the Quarterly Conference, his credentials may be restored to him.

PART IV.

EDUCATIONAL AND BENEVOLENT INSTITUTIONS.

Education.

¶ **247.** In order that the Church may provide for the higher education of her youth :—

§ 1. It is recommended that wherever practicable each Conference have at least one academy or seminary under its direct supervision; and that such institutions confine themselves to their legitimate sphere of duties.

§ 2. It is also recommended that, as a general thing, not less than four Conferences unite in the support of a college or university; and the Conferences are earnestly advised not to multiply schools, especially of this higher grade, beyond the wants of the people, or their ability to sustain them.

§ 3. All these schools are, to a certain extent, beneficiary institutions. The academy must be furnished with buildings and apparatus by the benevolence of the Church. The college must, in addition to these, have such endowment as shall yield a regular income sufficient to meet its current expenses; and, that our people may be properly instructed in this matter, it shall be the duty of each Preacher in Charge to preach on the subject of education once a year; to diffuse information by the distribution of tracts, or otherwise; and especially to call the attention of our wealthy members and friends to the duty of making liberal donations and bequests to this object.

§ 4. It shall be the duty of each Preacher in Charge of a Circuit or Station to take one public collection annually in each Society in aid of the work of education. The money so received shall be paid over to such auxiliary of the Board of Education as the Annual Conference may direct, or in the absence of Annual Conference directions to the Treasury of the Parent Board.

§ 5. It is recommended that the second Sunday in June be every-where observed as "Children's Day," and that wherever practicable a collection be taken in the Sunday-school in aid of the "Sunday-school Fund" of the Board of Education.

§ 6. It shall be the duty of each Presiding Elder to bring the subject of Education, in individual Churches, before the first Quarterly Conference of each year, and said Quarterly Conference shall appoint a Committee, of which the Preacher in Charge shall be *ex-officio* Chairman, to organize, wherever practicable, a Church Lyceum, under the supervision of the Quarterly Conference, for mental improvement, and to develop facilities for social intercourse; to organize free evening schools; to provide a library, text-books, and books of reference; to popularize religious literature, by reading-rooms or otherwise; to seek out suitable persons, and if necessary assist them to obtain an education, with a view to the Ministry; and to do whatever shall seem best fitted to supply any deficiency in that which the Church ought to offer to the varied nature of man.

Sunday-Schools and the Instruction of Children.

¶ **248.** For the moral and religious instruction of our children, and for the promotion of Bible knowledge among all our people:—

§ 1. Every Sunday-school of the Methodist Episcopal Church shall be under the supervision of a Sunday-school Board, and shall be auxiliary to the Sunday-school Union of the Methodist Episcopal Church.

§ 2. The Sunday-school Board shall consist of the Preacher in Charge, the Sunday-school Committee appointed by the Quarterly Conference, the Superintendent, the Assistant Superintendents, the Secretary, the Treasurer, the Librarians, and the Teachers of the school.

§ 3. The Superintendent shall be nominated and elected by the Sunday-school Board, and approved by the Quarterly Conference at its next session after such election.

§ 4. The other officers of the school shall be elected by the Sunday-school Board.

§ 5. The teachers of the school shall be nominated by the Superintendent, with the concurrence of the pastor, and elected by the Board.

§ 6. In case of the withdrawal of officers or teachers from the school they cease to be members of the Board; and the place of any officer or teacher habitually neglecting his or her duty, or being guilty of improper conduct, may be declared vacant by a vote of two thirds of the Board present at any regular or special meeting.

¶ **249.** It shall be the duty of each Presiding Elder to bring the subject of Sunday-schools before the last Quarterly Conference of each year; and said Quarterly Conference shall proceed to appoint a Committee of not less than three nor more than nine, who shall be members of our Church, to be called the Committee on Sunday-schools, of which the Preacher in Charge shall be the Chairman, who shall be members of the Sunday-school Board, and whose duty it shall be to aid the Preacher in Charge and the Officers of the Sunday-schools in procuring suitable teachers, in promoting in all proper ways the attendance of children and adults on our Sunday-schools and on our regular public worship, and in raising money to meet the expenses of the Sunday-schools of the charge.

¶ **250.** It shall be the duty of the Preacher in Charge, aided by the Superintendent and the Committee on Sunday-schools, to decide as to what books shall be used in our Sunday-schools.

¶ **251.** It shall be the special duty of the Preachers having charge of Circuits or Stations, with the aid of the other Preachers and the Committee on Sunday-schools, to form Sunday-schools in all our congregations where ten persons can be collected for that purpose, which schools shall be auxiliary to the Sunday-school Union of the Methodist Episcopal Church; and to engage the co-operation of as many of our members as they can, and to visit the schools as often as practicable; to preach on the subject of Sunday-schools and religious instruction in each congregation at least once in six months; and to form classes, wherever they can, for the instruction of the larger children, youth, and adults, in the word of God; and where they cannot superintend them personally, to see that suitable teachers are provided for that purpose.

¶ **252.** It shall be the duty of our

Preachers to enforce faithfully upon parents and Sunday-school teachers the great importance of instructing children in the doctrines and duties of our holy religion; to see that our Catechisms be used as extensively as possible in our Sunday-schools and families; to preach to the children and catechise them publicly in the Sunday-schools and at public meetings appointed for that purpose.

¶ 253. It shall be the duty of every Preacher, in his pastoral visits, to pay special attention to the children; to speak to them personally and kindly on the subject of experimental and practical godliness, according to their capacity; to pray earnestly for them; and diligently instruct and exhort all parents to dedicate their children to the Lord in baptism as early as convenient.

¶ 254. Each Preacher in Charge shall lay before the Quarterly Conference, to be entered on its journal, the number, state, and average attendance of the Sunday-schools in his charge, and the extent to which he has preached to the children and catechised them, and make the required report on Sunday-schools to his Annual Conference.

Missions and Missionary Societies.

¶ **255.** For the better prosecution of Missionary work in the United States and foreign countries, there shall be a Missionary Society, duly incorporated according to law, and having its office in the city of New York, said Society being subject to such rules and regulations as the General Conference may from time to time prescribe.

¶ **256.** It shall be the duty of each Annual Conference to form within its bounds a Conference Missionary Society, which shall appoint its own officers, fix the terms of membership, and otherwise regulate its own administration. But it shall pay all its funds into the treasury of the Parent Society.

¶ **257.** Any Annual Conference may, at its option, by a vote of two thirds of its members, assume the responsibility of supporting such Missions, already established within its own limits, as have hitherto been reported under the head of "Missions in the Destitute Portions of the Regular Work;" and for this purpose it shall be at liberty to organize a Conference Domestic Missionary Society, with branches *provided*, such organization shall not interfere with the collections for the Missionary Society of the Methodist Episcopal Church, as required by the Discipline. *Provided, also*, that in case more funds shall be raised for such Missions than are needed, the surplus shall be paid over to the Treasurer of the Missionary Society of the Methodist Episcopal Church, at New York, to be appropriated to such Mission or Missions, under the care of the Society, as may be designated by such Conference.

¶ **258.** It shall be the duty of the Preacher in Charge to see that each Sunday-school in our Churches and congregations be organized into a Missionary Society, under such rules and regulations as the Pastor, the Superintendent, and the Teachers may prescribe. And the Missionary contributions of the Sunday-schools shall be reported in a separate column in the benevolent contributions of the Annual and General Minutes.

¶ **259.** When a Mission is established in a foreign country, the Bishop having episcopal supervision of the same shall appoint a member of the mission as Superintendent, said Superintendent holding the relation in all ecclesiastical matters of a Presiding Elder in a District. It shall also be the duty of the Superintendent to represent the state of the Mission and its needs to the Bishop in charge and to the Corresponding Secretaries.

¶ 260. It shall be the duty of the Superintendent annually to call together all the members of the Mission, and also native preachers, of whatever grade, employed in the Mission, for the purpose of holding an annual meeting, said meeting possessing, in all ecclesiastical matters, the prerogatives and privileges of a District Conference, and also transacting such other business as may be assigned by the Board, or grow out of the local interests of the work.

¶ 261. When a Mission in a foreign country shall be organized into an Annual Conference, the administration of the Missionary Society is not thereby disturbed, but shall be continued as in the case of other Foreign Missions.

¶ 262. It shall be the duty of each Annual Conference within the bounds of the United States, where Missions have been, or are to be, established, to appoint a Standing Committee, (which shall keep a record of its doings and report the same to its Conference,) whose duty it shall be, with the concurrence of the President of the Conference, to make an estimate of the amount necessary for the support of each Mission and Mission-school, in full, or supplementary to the amount raised by the Society or Congregation thus aided; for which amount the President of the Conference for the time being shall draw on the Treasurer of the Society in quarterly installments.

¶ **263.** The support of Missions is committed to the Churches, Congregations, and Societies as such.

¶ **264.** It shall be the duty of each Presiding Elder to bring the subject of our Missions before the Quarterly Conference of each Circuit and Station within the District at the last Quarterly Conference in each year; and said Conference shall proceed to appoint a committee of not less than three nor more than nine, (of which the Preacher in Charge shall be chairman,) to be called the Committee on Missions, whose duty it shall be to aid the Preacher in Charge in carrying into effect the Disciplinary measures for the support of our Missions.

¶ **265.** It shall be the duty of each Presiding Elder to see that the provisions of this section are faithfully executed in his District, and in order thereto he shall inquire at each session of the Quarterly Conference what has been done by the Mission Committee toward raising funds for the support of Missions during the preceding quarter, and particularly whether the Sunday-schools have been organized into Missionary Societies.

¶ **266.** It shall be the duty of the Preacher in Charge, aided by the Committee on Missions, to provide for the diffusion of Missionary intelligence to the Church and Congregation.

¶ **267.** It shall be the duty of the Preacher in Charge, aided by the Committee on Missions, to institute a monthly missionary prayer meeting or lecture in each Society, or Church and Congregation, wherever practicable, for the purpose of imploring the Divine blessing on missions, for the diffusion of Missionary intelligence, and to afford an opportunity for voluntary offerings to the Missionary cause.

¶ **268.** It shall be the duty of the Preacher in Charge, aided by the Committee on Missions, to appoint Missionary Collectors, and furnish them with suitable books and instructions, that they may call on each member of the Society, or Church and Congregation, and on other persons, at their discretion, for his or her annual, semi-annual, quarterly, monthly, or weekly contribution for the support of missions. Said Collectors shall make monthly returns (unless otherwise instructed by the Committee) to the Preacher in Charge, or to the Missionary Treasurer of the Church, if there be such Treasurer appointed by the Committee on Missions. Such returns shall be entered in a book, which the committee shall provide, together with collections and contributions received from other sources. Such entries shall set forth the name of each Collector, the real or assumed names of the contributors, and the amount contributed by each.

¶ **269.** Each Preacher in Charge shall report at Conference to the Executive Committee, or the Board of Managers of the Conference Missionary Society, a plain transcript of the record of the returns provided for in ¶ 268, comprehending the name of each Collector in his charge, and the name, real or assumed, of each contributor to each Collector, that they may be arranged by districts and by charges for publication in the annual report of the Conference Missionary Society, together with the contributions and collections received from other sources, unless the Conference shall by vote declare such transcript returns and such publications unadvisable.

¶ **270.** It shall be the duty of the Preacher in Charge, with the aid of the Committee on Missions, to present once in the year to each congregation the cause of Missions, and to ask public collections and contributions for the support of the same. The manner of asking and taking such collections and contributions shall be at the discretion of the Pastor and the Committee on Missions, with this injunction, that the Pastor shall preach, or cause to be preached on the occasion, one or more sermons, and with the recommendation that one whole Sabbath day be given to the cause on this annual presentation of Missions in our principal Churches and Congregations.

¶ **271.** The President of the Conference, at each session, shall appoint one of its members, with an alternate, to preach a Missionary sermon during its next succeeding session, at such time and place as the officers of the Conference Missionary Society shall designate; and said officers shall cause timely notice of said sermon to be published abroad.

¶ **272.** When the character of the Presiding Elder is under examination, the Bishop shall ask him whether the provisions of the Discipline for the support of Missions have been carried out in his District; and when the character of a Preacher in Charge is examined, he shall inquire of him what amount has been raised on his charge for Missions.

¶ **273.** Each Corresponding Secretary of the Missionary Society of the Methodist Episcopal Church shall be a member of such Annual Conference as he may, with the approbation of the Bishops, select.

¶ **274.** The Board of Managers of the Missionary Society shall have power to suspend a Corresponding Secretary, or Treasurer, or Manager, for cause to them sufficient, and a time shall be fixed by the Board, at as early a day as practicable, for the investigation of the official conduct of said Secretary, Treasurer, or Manager, due notice of which shall be given by them to the Bishops, who shall select one of their number to be present and preside at the investigation, which shall be before the twelve members of the General Missionary Committee elected from the Districts by the General Conference, two thirds of whom may remove said Secretary, Treasurer, or Manager from office in the interval of the General Conference.

¶ 275. In case a vacancy exists in the office of Corresponding Secretary, Treasurer, or Assistant Treasurer, by death, resignation, or otherwise, the Bishops shall have power to fill the vacancy; and until they do so, the Board of Managers shall have power to provide for the duties of the office. It shall be the duty of the General Missionary Committee to revise annually the lists of Managers, and in any case of inattention to the duties of the office, they may declare the said Manager's seat vacant.

Board of Church Extension.

¶ 276. There shall be a Board of Church Extension, consisting of thirty-two Ministers and thirty-two Laymen, to be chosen by the General Conference, and to be duly incorporated according to law, with such powers and prerogatives as may be needful to the objects of its appointment; said Board to be subject to the control of the General Conference. The Bishops shall be *ex-officio* members of the Board.

¶ 277. The term of service of the members of the Board shall begin on the first day of January following their appointment, and continue during the ensuing four years, and until their successors shall be duly chosen and have entered upon their duties, unless otherwise ordered by the General Conference. If a vacancy should occur by death, resignation, or otherwise, during the interval of the General Conference, the Board shall have power to fill the vacancy.

¶ 278. The Officers of the Board shall be a President, five Vice-Presidents, a Corresponding Secretary, with such Assistants as the General Committee of Church Extension may authorize and appoint, a Recording Secretary, Treasurer, and Assistant Treasurer, all of whom, except the Corresponding Secretary and Assistants, shall be elected by the Board at the first regular meeting in January of each year.

¶ 279. The Corresponding Secretary shall be appointed by the General Conference, and shall be a member of such Conference as he, with the approval of the Bishops, may select. He shall conduct the correspondence of the Board, under its direction, and shall be subject to the authority and control of the Board, by whom his salary shall be fixed and paid. He shall be exclusively employed in conducting the affairs of the Board, and, under its direction, in promoting its general interest, by traveling or otherwise. Should a vacancy occur by death, resignation, or otherwise, the Board shall have power to provide for the duties of the office until the Bishops, or a majority of them, shall fill the vacancy.

¶ 280. An Assistant Corresponding Secretary, or more than one, may be appointed at any time by the General Committee, on the nomination of the Bishops, who shall receive such salary, and render such service, as the Board may determine.

¶ 281. The Board shall hold its meetings in the city of Philadelphia. It shall have authority to make by-laws for the regulation of its own proceedings; to provide for and administer a Loan Fund; to take and hold in trust for the Methodist Episcopal Church any real or personal property, and to dispose of the same for the use and benefit of the Church; and generally to do all and singular the matters and things which shall be necessary and lawful in the execution of its trusts: *provided, however*, that all amounts received on the Loan Fund shall be used only by loans on adequate security; and *provided*, further, that the aggregate amount of interest and annuities payable shall never be allowed to exceed the aggregate amount of interest receivable.

¶ 282. The Board shall also have authority to provide and recommend a uniform plan for the organization of local boards of Church Extension in large cities, under such local administration as may be deemed advisable; but in no case shall such local organization interfere with the general work of the Board.

¶ 283. The Board shall also have authority, by constituting and procuring a special corporation, or otherwise, to take such measures as it may deem wise and necessary to procure the insurance of churches and other church property against loss by fire; and the profits arising therefrom, if any, after the accumulation of a sufficient reserve fund, shall be devoted to the purposes of the Board.

¶ 284. The Board shall also have authority, with the concurrence of the General Committee, to make such provisions as it may deem wise for honorary membership in the Parent and Conference Boards of Church Extension, and in the General Committee.

¶ 285. At all meetings of the Board thirteen members shall constitute a quorum.

¶ 286. The minutes of each meeting shall be signed by the Secretary thereof.

¶ 287. The Board shall publish annually a full report of its proceedings, and of the state of its funds, and shall submit to the General Conference an abstract of the same for the preceding four years.

¶ 288. Each Annual Conference shall, on the nomination of the Presiding Bishop and Presiding Elders, appoint a Conference Board of Church Extension, composed of equal numbers of Ministers and Laymen, consisting of a President, Vice-

President, Recording Secretary, Corresponding Secretary, and Treasurer, and not less than three nor more than seven additional members, so located that a quorum thereof may be convened at any time. And the Secretary of the Conference shall notify the Corresponding Secretary of the Parent Board of the name and post-office address of each member thereof.

¶ 289. The Conference Board shall be auxiliary to the Parent Board, and shall, under its direction, have charge of all the interests and work of Church Extension within the Conference. It shall see that the amount asked of the Conference by the General Committee is divided for collection among the several Districts and Pastoral Charges with due regard to their circumstances and ability, and that each is notified early in the year; and shall, in connection with the Conference, take all necessary measures to secure at least the amount so asked, and special donations and bequests to the Loan Fund.

¶ 290. The Conference Board shall carefully examine all applications for aid from within the bounds of the Conference, and recommend only such as are found to be truly needy and meritorious. It shall keep and preserve in suitable books, to be furnished by the Parent Board, a faithful record of all its proceedings, and an account of amounts asked and received each year from every Pastoral Charge; and shall make full report thereof to each session of the Annual Conference for publication in the Conference Minutes, and at the same time to the Parent Board.

¶ 291. The Treasurer of the Conference Board shall, as early as practicable, at least once in every three months, remit all funds coming into his hands to the Treasurer of the Parent Board.

¶ 292. If for any reason such Conference Board cannot be constituted or act, the Bishop having charge, or a Committee by him appointed, may perform any of the duties required in this section.

¶ 293. There shall be a General Committee of Church Extension, composed as follows,—1. The General Superintendents, one of whom, as they may from time to time determine, shall be Chairman. 2. The Corresponding Secretary and Assistants, Recording Secretary, who shall be *ex-officio* Secretary of the Committee, and the Treasurer of the Board.

3. The Annual Conferences being grouped by the General Conference into Twelve Church Extension Districts, there shall be one member from each District elected by the General Conference on the nomination of the Delegates of each District respectively, and a corresponding number appointed by the Board.

¶ **294.** It shall be the duty of this Committee to meet annually in the City of Philadelphia, on such day in the month of November as shall be appointed by the Corresponding Secretary, to determine,—1. What amount each Conference shall be asked to raise by collections for the use of the Board during the ensuing year; 2. What amount may be donated and loaned within each Conference during the same period; and 3. What amount may be applied to general and special purposes not included in the above.

¶ **295.** The General Committee shall also have authority to counsel and direct the Board in the general administration of the trust committed to its care.

¶ **296.** If a vacancy should occur in the Committee by death, resignation, removal from the District, or otherwise, the Bishop having charge of the Conference within which it occurs shall fill the vacancy.

¶ **297**. Expenses incurred by the Committee in the discharge of its duties may be paid by the Treasurer of the Board.

¶ **298**. All applications for aid shall be made in accordance with blank forms, to be furnished by the Parent Board, and shall set forth,—1. The number of Church members, Sunday-school children, and congregation to be accommodated, the population of the place, and prospects of growth. 2. The legal incorporation of the Church or Board of Trustees. 3. The location, size, present and prospective value of the site, the validity of the title thereto, and whether held in trust for the Methodist Episcopal Church. 4. A description of the building to which aid, if granted, will be applied; and, if required, a copy of the plans and specifications of the architect shall be submitted, and, if deemed necessary by the Parent or Conference Board, modified as may be suggested. 5. The estimated and probable cost when completed. 6. The available resources and amount of reliable subscriptions; and that those immediately interested have done or are doing all that could reasonably be expected. 7. What amount of debt, if any, may be allowed to remain against the property, and how soon the Trustees or others will agree to remove it. 8. Is the property insured? Will it be? In what company? To what amount? 9. Whether the Church, if aided, will become self-supporting, and how soon, and to what extent it may be expected to aid in the general work of the Church. 10. Any additional facts and circumstances that will assist the Board to a proper decision on the application.

¶ 299. Every such application for aid shall be first submitted to the Conference Board of Church Extension, and said Board shall certify its action thereon to the Parent Board, and aid shall be granted only by the concurrent action of both the Conference and Parent Boards, and, except in cases of great emergency, within the amount authorized by the General Committee: *provided*, however, that for the procurement of property in mission territory the Parent Board may appropriate funds specially authorized by the General Committee without such application or recommendation by a Conference Board; but in all such cases the title to such property should vest in the Board of Church Extension.

¶ 300. It shall be the duty of each Presiding Elder to bring the subject of Church Extension before the Quarterly Conference of each Circuit and Station within his District at the last Quarterly Conference in each year; and said Quarterly Conference shall appoint a Committee of not less than three nor more than five, of which the Preacher in Charge shall be Chairman, to be called the Committee on Church Extension, whose duty it shall be to aid the Preacher in Charge in carrying into effect the provisions of the Discipline and plans of the Boards for the support of this cause, and in securing at least the amount asked of the Circuit or Station for its aid; and the Presiding Elder shall inquire, in the third Quarterly Conference of each year, what has been done for this cause, and whether the amount asked has been received, and if not, he shall urgently request the Preacher in Charge and the Quarterly Conference to take such measures as will secure it before the close of the year.

¶ 301. It shall be the duty of the Preacher in Charge, aided by the Committee on Church Extension, to provide for the diffusion of information concerning the work and wants of the Board of Church Extension; he shall preach, or cause to be preached, a sermon on this subject in each congregation in every year, and solicit contributions from each, endeavoring to secure at least the amount asked as above provided; and shall at each Conference report the amount asked, and the amount received, for Church Extension. He shall also invite special contributions and bequests to the Loan Fund.

Freedmen's Aid.

¶ 302. For the mental and moral elevation of Freedmen and others in the South who have special claims upon the Christian people of America:—

§ 1. Let all our people contribute liberally each year for the support of our Freedmen's Aid Society.

§ 2. Let the Freedmen's Aid Society be careful to locate its schools where they will be of most advantage to our Churches and Missions, and especially seek to educate those persons who are called to preach, or who propose to become preachers; and let only those persons be employed as teachers who will conscientiously work in our Sunday-schools, and cheerfully co-operate with our ministers.

¶ **303.** The Board of Managers shall determine what amount shall be expended annually in this work, and apportion the same, according to their best judgment, among the several Annual Conferences; and each Annual Conference shall apportion, or cause to be apportioned, the amount assigned to it among the Circuits and Stations within its bounds; and each Presiding Elder, as early in the Conference year as possible, shall inform each Quarterly Conference in his District of the amount to be raised by the Charge it represents.

¶ **304.** It shall be the duty of each Preacher in Charge to present this subject to his congregation, or cause it to be presented, once each year in a sermon or address; to aid in the diffusion of intelligence in regard to the work of the Society and the wants of the Freedmen, and to use due diligence to collect the amount apportioned to his Charge. He shall report to the Annual Conference the sum collected, and the collections shall be published in a column in the General Minutes and in the Minutes of the Annual Conferences.

¶ 305. The Corresponding Secretary, if a Traveling Preacher, shall be a member of such Annual Conference as he, with the approbation of the Bishops, may select.

Circulation of Religious Tracts.

¶ 306. It is recommended to our people every-where to form Tract Societies, auxiliary to the Tract Society of the Methodist Episcopal Church.

¶ 307. It is recommended to Preachers in Charge to make annually, in their several congregations, collections in behalf of the Tract Society of the Methodist Episcopal Church.

¶ 308. It shall be the duty of each Presiding Elder to bring the Tract cause before the last Quarterly Meeting Conference of each year, in each Circuit and Station within his District; and said Conference shall appoint a Committee whose duty it shall be to devise and execute plans for local tract distribution.

Printing and Circulating Books, Tracts, and Periodicals.

¶ 309. The principal Publishing Houses of the Book Concern shall be in the cities of New York and Cincinnati; but there shall be depositories of our publications at such other places as the General Conference may from time to time determine.

¶ 310. The General Conference shall quadrennially elect two Agents for the Publishing House in New York, and two Agents for that in Cincinnati, who shall have authority, and whose duty it shall be, under the supervision of the Book Committee, to regulate the publications and all other parts of the business of the Concern (except what belongs to the editorial departments) in such manner as the state of the finances will admit, and the interests of the Church may require; and who, if chosen from among the Traveling Preachers, shall be members of such Annual Conferences as they may, with the approbation of the Bishops, select.

¶ 311. It shall be the duty of the Agents of both Publishing Houses to publish such books, tracts, periodicals, etc., as are ordered or recommended by the General Conference; also, to publish such as are recommended by the Book Committee, and approved by the Book Editors; and they may reprint any book or tract which has been once approved and published by us, when, in their judgment and that of the Book Editors, the same ought to be reprinted; and they may publish any new work which the Book Editors may approve.

¶ 312. The Agents of the Western Publishing House at Cincinnati shall supervise and manage the business of the Western country in co-operation with the Agents at New York; they shall have authority to publish any book or tract which has been previously published by the Agents at New York, when, in their judgment and in that of the Book Committee, the demand for such publication will justify and the interest of the Church require such re-publication; and the Agents at New York shall fill the orders of the Agents at Cincinnati for the plates of such books or tracts; and when the

Agents at New York are about to issue any new work, they shall, when practicable, furnish to the Agents at Cincinnati, if ordered by them, duplicate plates, which, with the above, shall be at cost: *provided*, however, that the Agents at Cincinnati shall not reprint our large works, such as Commentaries, Quarto Bibles, Wesley's and Fletcher's Works, or any other works of more than seven hundred pages.

¶ 313. Printed sheets ordered by the Cincinnati Agents from New York shall be sent at fifty per cent., and bound books of the General Catalogue at forty per cent. discount from the retail prices, and those ordered from Cincinnati to New York shall be sent on the same terms: the Publishing House sending the books to be charged with the expenses of transportation. The Agents at Cincinnati shall remit to the Agents at New York during the current year as largely and frequently as their funds will allow; and if practicable, to the full amount of stock furnished; they shall also pay one third of all the appropriations made by the General Conference, unless the said Conference shall otherwise order.

¶ 314. The Agents at each Publishing

House shall keep a separate account with each department of the business, and with each periodical published, under their supervision; and they shall set forth in their Reports to the Annual and General Conferences the amount of sales, receipts, and expenditures for books, periodicals, and depositories under their control, with whatever profits or losses may have accrued on each. They shall furnish to the local Sub-Committee hereinafter designated, at each of its monthly meetings, a full and satisfactory statement of the transactions of the preceding month; and, if the Sub-Committee shall so require, furnish for examination vouchers for all payments made during the period specified; and they shall give to the said Sub-Committee at each of the monthly meetings every possible means and facility for a full and intelligent understanding of all the business transactions of the Concern.

¶ 315. The Agents, both at New York and Cincinnati, shall annually take an account of stock, including in their inventory all the property and assets of the respective Publishing Houses, at their estimated cash value, except real estate, which shall have a value estimated by the Book Committee at the beginning of each quadrennium, which shall not be changed during the quadrennium except by the necessary changes caused by the purchase or sale, improvement or destruction, of real estate; together with a full and detailed statement of all their liabilities, profits, and losses; and they shall always hand over to their successors in office such a statement of stock, property, assets, and liabilities, as shall be approved and certified by the Book Committee.

¶ **316.** The Book Agents and Editors are required to give their undivided attention to the duties of their respective positions, and to require of their *employés* the faithful discharge of the work assigned them.

¶ **317.** The General Conference shall elect a Book Committee of eighteen members, to serve for four years, consisting of one from each of the twelve Districts into which the Annual Conferences are distributed, and of three from New York or its vicinity, and three from Cincinnati or vicinity; which Committee shall, during the interval of the General

Conference, have power to fill vacancies occurring in its own body. Such Committee shall have the general supervision of the publishing interests of the Church examine carefully into their condition, and make report of the same to the Annual Conferences and to the General Conference; and shall also attend to all matters referred to it by the Agents or Editors for its action or counsel.

¶ 318. The three members at New York and the three at Cincinnati shall have power to suspend an Agent or Editor for cause to them sufficient, and a time shall be fixed at as early a day as practicable for the investigation of the official conduct of said Agent or Editor, due notice of which shall be given by the Chairman of the Book Committee to the Bishops, who shall select one of their number to be present and preside at the investigation, which shall be before the twelve members from the Districts into which the Annual Conferences are distributed, two thirds of whom may remove said Agent or Editor from office in the interval of the General Conference. And in case a vacancy occurs in any of the agencies or editorial departments authorized by the General Conference, it shall be the duty of the Book Committee, and two or more of the General Superintendents, as soon as practicable, to provide for such vacancy until the next General Conference.

¶ 319. The Book Committee shall be governed by the following regulations: —

§ 1. Immediately after its appointment the members shall divide themselves into two sections of nine each, the one to consist of the members from the Eastern Districts, together with those chosen from New York and vicinity, to be called the Eastern Section; the other to consist of the members from the Western Districts, and those chosen from Cincinnati and vicinity, to be called the Western Section.

§ 2. To the Eastern Section shall pertain the supervision of the New York Publishing House in all its departments. The three members chosen from New York and vicinity shall constitute a local Sub-Committee, which shall meet monthly at the Book Room in New York, to examine into all the transactions of the month preceding; it shall keep a correct record of its proceedings, to be submitted to the Eastern Section of the Book Committee, at its annual meeting, to be held at the place of, and on the day previous to, the meeting of the Book Committee.

§ 3. The Western Section of the Book Committee shall perform the same duties for the Publishing House at Cincinnati, and be under the same regulations, as are herein specified for the government of the Eastern Section.

§ 4. The annual meeting of the Book Committee shall be held on the second Wednesday of February; and each section shall have meetings at such time as it may elect.

¶ **320.** There shall be elected by the General Conference, to serve for four years, the following Editors:—The Editor of the "Quarterly Review," who shall also be the Editor of the Books of the General Catalogue; the Editor of Sunday-school Books, Papers, and Tracts, at New York; the Editor of the "Christian Advocate," at New York; the Editor of the "Pittsburgh Christian Advocate," at Pittsburgh, Pa.; the Editor of the "Northern Christian Advocate," at Syracuse, New York; the Editor of the

"California Christian Advocate," at San Francisco, Cal.; the Editor of the "Pacific Christian Advocate," at Portland, Oregon; and an Editor of the "Southwestern Christian Advocate," at New Orleans; also, an Editor of the "Western Christian Advocate," an Editor of the "Ladies' Repository" and "Golden Hours," who shall be Editor of the Books of the General Catalogue and Tracts; an Editor of the "Christian Apologist," and German Books of the General Catalogue; an Editor of the German "Monthly Family Magazine," "Sunday-School Bell," "Family Library," Tracts, and other German Sunday-school publications, all of which shall be published at Cincinnati; an Editor of the "Northwestern Christian Advocate," at Chicago; an Editor of the "Central Christian Advocate," at St. Louis, Mo.; an Editor of the "Methodist Advocate," at Atlanta, Ga.; who, if chosen from among the Traveling Preachers, shall be members of such Annual Conferences as they, with the approbation of the Bishops, may select. The officers mentioned in this chapter shall be either ministers or members of the Methodist Episcopal Church.

¶ 321. The Editor of Sunday-school Books, Papers, and Tracts shall also have charge of all our Tract Publications, and shall be Corresponding Secretary of the Tract Society. He shall also, in consultation with the Book Agents, have charge of the department of Sunday-school Requisites, including books of instruction for Sunday-schools and Normal Classes. He shall also be Corresponding Secretary of the Sunday-school Union and Superintendent of the Department of Sunday-school Instruction. The Tract Society and the Sunday-school Union shall each pay such proportion of his salary as the Book Committee, in consultation with the Executive Committee of each Society, shall consider just, in view of the time spent by the Secretary in the service of each Society.

¶ 322. Every Annual Conference shall appoint a Committee, which, in the absence of the Agent, shall attend to the collection of the accounts sent out from the Book Concern, and return an accurate report of the same.

¶ 323. Every Presiding Elder, Minister, and Preacher shall do every thing in his power to recover all debts due to the Concern for books or periodicals, within the bounds of his Charge. If any person, Preacher, or Member, be indebted to the Book Concern, and refuse or neglect to make payment, or to come to a just settlement, let him be dealt with in the same manner as is directed in other cases of debt and disputed accounts.

¶ 324. There shall be a Publishing Committee at San Francisco, to consist of three Ministers and two Laymen, appointed by the General Conference, whose powers with respect to the Depository and the paper at San Francisco shall be the same as those of the General Book Committee. Said Committee may nominate an Agent for the Depository, subject to the approval of the Book Agents at New York.

¶ 325. There shall also be a Publishing Committee for the "Pittsburgh Christian Advocate" at Pittsburgh, Pa., and a Publishing Committee for the "Pacific Christian Advocate" at Portland, Oregon, whose respective duties with regard to these papers shall be similar to the duties of the Book Agents and Book Committee, in relation to the publications under their care, so far as they may be applicable to the establishments under their supervision.

¶ 326. The Publishing Committee of the "Pittsburgh Christian Advocate" shall consist of three members from the Pittsburgh Conference, two from the Erie Conference, two from the East Ohio Conference, and two from the West Virginia Conference, to be chosen by the General Conference.

¶ 327. The Oregon Annual Conference shall annually choose a Publishing Committee of five persons for the "Pacific Christian Advocate," which Committee shall also exercise general supervision of the affairs of the Depository at Portland.

¶ 328. The Publishing Committee in each of these establishments shall keep an account of the receipts and expenditures for the paper; correspond with the Agents at New York; hold all moneys, after defraying current expenses, subject to their order; and shall report annually on the state of the establishment to their Conference or Conferences, and to the Agents at New York. And whenever it shall be found that such papers do not fully support themselves with such aid as may have been allowed them, it shall be the duty of the Publishing Committee to discontinue them.

¶ **329.** There shall be a Depository of our books at Pittsburgh, Pennsylvania; at Boston, Massachusetts; at Buffalo, New York; and at San Francisco, California, furnished by the Agents at New York with full supplies of the books of our General Catalogue, Sunday-school books, and Tracts, to be sold for the Concern on the same terms as at New York: *provided*, that there shall not be more than fifteen thousand dollars' worth at Pittsburgh, nor more than ten thousand dollars' worth at Boston. There shall also be a Depository at Chicago, Illinois; one at St. Louis, Missouri; and one at Atlanta, Georgia, to be supplied by the Agents at Cincinnati.

¶ **330.** The expenses incident to the transportation, management, and sale of our books at these Depositories having been met out of the sales, according to an arrangement with the Agents, the net proceeds shall be forwarded to said Agents as fast as possible.

¶ **331.** Full statements shall be made

to the Agents semi-annually, at dates fixed by them, of the amount of sales, and of expenses; distinguishing cash sales from those on credit. And, also, annual statements shall be made of the amount of stock.

¶ **332.** If it shall appear to the Agents that the business at either of the Depositories is not well managed, or that remittances are not duly made, they shall immediately correct the error complained of; or, with the concurrence of the Book Committee, cause the affairs of the Depository to be wound up.

¶ **333.** No books shall hereafter be sold on commission either from New York, Cincinnati, or any other depository or establishment under our direction.

¶ **334.** The salaries of the Editors and Agents at New York, and of the "Northern Christian Advocate," the salaries of the Agents and Editors at Cincinnati, and of the Editors at Chicago, St. Louis, Atlanta, and New Orleans, shall be fixed by the Book Committee. The salaries of the Editors of the papers at Pittsburgh, Pennsylvania, at San Francisco, California, and at Portland, Oregon, shall be fixed by the Publishing Committees having charge of those papers respectively. The amounts to be appropriated for Correspondence shall also be fixed by the Book Committee.

¶ **335.** The profits arising from the Book Concern, after a sufficient capital to carry on the business is retained, shall be regularly applied to the support of the deficient Traveling Preachers and their families, the widows and orphans of Preachers, etc. The Book Agents shall every year send forward to each Annual Conference an account of the dividend which the several Annual Conferences may draw that year, and each Conference may draw for its proportionate part on any person who has book money in hand; and the drafts, with the receipt of the Conference thereon, shall be sent to the Book Agents, and be placed to the credit of the person who paid the same.

¶ **336.** The Annual Conferences are affectionately and earnestly requested not to establish any more Conference papers; and where such papers exist, they may be discontinued when it can be done consistently with existing obligations.

¶ **337.** Any Traveling Preacher, who

may publish any work or book of his own, shall be responsible to his Conference for any obnoxious matter or doctrine therein contained.

The Chartered Fund.

¶ 338. To make further provision for the distressed Traveling Preachers, for the families of Traveling Preachers, and for the Superannuated and Worn-out Preachers, and the widows and orphans of Preachers, there shall be a Chartered Fund, to be supported by the voluntary contributions of our friends; the principal stock of which shall be funded under the direction of Trustees chosen by the General Conference, and the interest applied under the direction of the General Conference, according to the following regulations, namely:—

§ 1. The Elders, and those who have the oversight of Circuits, shall be collectors and receivers of subscriptions, etc., for this fund.

§ 2. The money shall, if possible, be conveyed by bills of exchange, or otherwise, through the means of the post, to the General Book Agents, who shall pay it to the Trustees of the fund; otherwise it shall be brought to the ensuing Annual Conference.

§ 3. The interest shall be divided into eighty-nine equal parts, and each of the Annual Conferences shall have authority to draw one of these parts out of the fund; and if one or more Conferences less than one of these parts be drawn out of the fund in any given year, then in such case or cases the other Annual Conferences, held in the same year, shall have authority, if they judge it necessary, to draw out of the fund such surplus of the interest which has not been applied by the former Conferences; and the Bishops shall bring the necessary information of the state of the interest of the fund, respecting the year in question, from Conference to Conference.

§ 4. All drafts on the Chartered Fund shall be made on the President of the said fund, by order of the Annual Conference, signed by the President and countersigned by the Secretary of the said Conference.

§ 5. The money subscribed for the Chartered Fund may be lodged, on proper securities, in the States respectively in which it has been subscribed, under the direction of deputies living in such States respectively; *provided*, such securities and such deputies be proposed as shall be approved of by the Trustees in Philadelphia, and the stock in which it is proposed to lodge the money be sufficiently productive to give satisfaction to the Trustees.

¶ **339.** The Board of Trustees shall have power to fill any vacancy or vacancies that may occur in their body by death, resignation, or otherwise, subject, however, to the approval of the first General Conference that may be held after such vacancy or vacancies shall have occurred.

The Permanent Fund.

¶ **340.** There shall be a fund known as "The Permanent Fund," to be held by the Trustees of the Methodist Episcopal Church, the principal of which shall be intact forever, and which shall be invested by said Trustees on first-class securities, and at as favorable rates as can be legally secured.

¶ **341.** It shall be the duty of all our

ministers to obtain, as far as practicable, contributions to said fund, by donations, bequests, and otherwise.

¶ 342. The interest accumulating from said fund shall be subject to the order of the General Conference for the following purposes:—1. To pay the expenses of the General Conference. 2. To pay the expenses of Delegations appointed by the General Conference to Corresponding Bodies. 3. To make up any deficiencies in the salaries of the Bishops. 4. To relieve the necessities of the Superannuated and Worn-out Preachers, and of the widows and orphans of those who have died in the work.

PART V.

TEMPORAL ECONOMY.

CHAPTER I.

SUPPORT OF MINISTERS.

The Support of Bishops, and the Families of Deceased Bishops.

¶ **343.** The General Conference shall determine which of the Bishops are effective, and which are non-effective.

¶ **344.** It shall be the duty of the Book Committee to make an estimate of the amount necessary to furnish a competent support to each effective Bishop, considering the number and condition of his family; and the amount, if any, necessary to the comfortable maintenance of the non-effective Bishops; and also the amount necessary to assist the widows and children of deceased Bishops; and the Bishops are authorized to draw on the Agents of the Book Concern for said amount, and also for their traveling expenses.*

* For action of the General Conference restricting the authority of the Agents to pay the drafts of the Bishops, see *Appendix*, No. 22, p. 383.

¶ **345.** The Bishop presiding at an Annual Conference, within whose bounds a widow or orphan of a deceased Bishop may reside, shall be authorized to draw on the Agents of the Book Concern for such amount as may be estimated as aforesaid.

¶ **346.** The Book Committee shall divide the aggregate sum required to be raised for these purposes among the Annual Conferences, according to their several ability; and the Annual Conferences shall apportion the same to the several Districts; and the District Stewards to the several charges. The amount apportioned to each Pastoral Charge for the support of the Bishops shall be a *pro rata* claim with that of the stationed Preachers and Presiding Elders, and no such Preacher or Presiding Elder shall be entitled to his allowance except to the extent to which the claims of the Bishops are met by the Station or District with which he is connected. And it shall be the duty of the Annual Conferences to see that the amounts apportioned to the different pastoral charges for the support of the Bishops are raised and forwarded quarterly, when practicable, to the Agents of the Book Concern.

¶ **347.** The Agents of the Book Concern shall charge the sums paid to the Bishops, and to the widows and children of deceased Bishops, to "The Episcopal Fund," and all collections received from the different charges for the support of the Bishops shall be credited to said fund. And the Agents shall report annually to the Annual Conferences the amounts received from the several Annual Conferences on account of said fund, and also the expenditures made; and shall make a full and detailed exhibit of such receipts and expenditures for the term of four years in their Quadrennial Report to the General Conference; and if there shall be a deficiency, and a balance due the Book Concern, the General Conference shall provide for its payment.

Support of Presiding Elders.

¶ **348.** There shall be annually, in every District, a meeting composed of one Steward from each Circuit and Station, to be selected by the Quarterly Conference, whose duty it shall be, with the advice of the Presiding Elder, (who shall preside in such meeting,) to make an estimate of the amount necessary to furnish a comfortable support to the Presiding Elder, and to apportion the same, including house-rent and traveling expenses, and also the claim of the Bishops assessed to the District by the Annual Conference, among the different Circuits and Stations in the District, according to their several ability; and in all cases the Presiding Elder shall share with the Preachers in his District in proportion with what they have respectively received; but if there be a surplus ot money raised for the support of the Preachers in one or more of the Circuits or Stations in his District, he shall receive such surplus, provided he do not receive more than his allowance.

Support of Ministers and Preachers.

¶ **349.** It shall be the duty of the Quarterly Conference of each Circuit and Station, at the session immediately preceding the Annual Conference, to appoint an Estimating Committee, consisting of three or more members of the

Church, who shall, after conferring with the Preachers, make an estimate of the amount necessary to furnish a comfortable support to the Preacher or Preachers stationed among them, taking into consideration the number and condition of the family or families of such Preacher or preachers, which estimate shall be subject to the action of the Quarterly Conference; and to which shall be added the amount apportioned for the support of the Bishops and Presiding Elder; and the Stewards shall provide by such methods as they may judge best to meet such amount. The traveling and moving expenses of the Preachers shall not be reckoned as a part of the estimate, but be paid by the Stewards separately.

¶ 350. Whenever a member of an Annual Conference applies for a location, it shall be asked, Is he indebted to the Book Concern? and if it be ascertained that he is, the Conference shall require him to secure said debt, if they judge it at all necessary or proper, before they grant him a location. Whenever any claimant on the funds of a Conference shall be in debt to the Book Concern, the Conference of which he is a member shall have power to appropriate the amount of such claim, or any part thereof, to the payment of said debt.

¶ **351.** When a member of an Annual Conference is accused of crime in the interval of his conference session, and is suspended by a Committee, and subsequently convicted by his Conference and expelled, his claim upon the funds of the Conference shall cease from the time of his suspension.

Support of Superannuated Preachers.

¶ **352.** It shall be the duty of the Quarterly Conference of each Charge within whose bounds a Superannuated Preacher, or the widow or child of a deceased Preacher, may reside, to appoint a Committee whose duty it shall be to make an estimate of the amount necessary to assist such Preacher, widow, or child in obtaining a comfortable support, and such estimate shall be sent up to the Annual Conference with which the claimant may be connected, and subject to the action of said Annual Conference.

Local Preachers to have an Allowance in Certain Cases.

¶ **353.** Whenever a Local Preacher fills the place of a Traveling Preacher, with the approbation of the Presiding Elder, he shall be paid for his time a sum proportional to the allowance of a Traveling Preacher; which sum shall be paid by the Circuit at the next Quarterly Meeting, if the Traveling Preacher whose place he filled up were either sick or necessarily absent; or, in other cases, out of the allowance of the Traveling Preacher.

¶ **354.** If a Local Preacher be distressed in his temporal circumstances on account of his service in the Circuit, he may apply to the Quarterly Conference, who may give him what relief they judge proper, after the allowance of the Traveling Preachers and of their wives, and all other regular allowances, are discharged.

PART V.—CHAPTER II.

RAISING SUPPLIES—PARSONAGES.

Methods for Raising Annual Supplies for the Propagation of the Gospel, and for making up the Allowance of Preachers.

¶ 355. The more effectually to raise the amount necessary to meet the above mentioned allowances of the effective Ministers and Preachers, let the Stewards at the beginning of the year estimate the amount needed monthly. Then ascertain from each member of the Church, and, as far as practicable, from each attendant of the congregation, what each purposes to give as his monthly contribution.

¶ 356. Let these sums be entered by the Recording Steward in a book which he shall keep as Treasurer of the Board of Stewards. If the total amount of these sums does not equal the amount needed monthly, then let the Stewards apportion the deficiency among all such as are willing, for Christ's sake, to assume such deficiency, setting down to each person, with his consent, the additional amount which they think he ought monthly to pay.

¶ 357. Let the Stewards then adopt and carry out a plan by which every one —except such as prefer to make weekly contributions through their Class Leaders —shall have the opportunity of regularly contributing each month, or oftener, not grudgingly nor of necessity, the sum which has been pledged by him. Let these contributions be paid over regularly to the Recording Steward or Class Leader, and be brought up by him to the Leaders and Stewards' Meeting or Quarterly Conference, as the case may be. The Recording Steward shall keep an individual account of all these pledges and contributions, and shall pay over the same, under the direction of the Stewards, to the Preachers authorized to receive them.

¶ 358. To provide to meet the claims that may be presented and determined at the Annual Conference, every Preacher shall make an annual collection in every congregation of his charge, and the money so collected shall be lodged in the hands of the Steward or Stewards, and brought or sent to the ensuing Annual Conference.

¶ **359.** Let the annual produce of the Chartered Fund, as divided among the several Annual Conferences, be applied with the above contributions, but so as not to militate against the rules of the Chartered Fund, and also the annual dividend arising from the profits of the Book Concern. Out of the money so collected and brought to the respective Annual Conferences, let the various allowances agreed upon in accordance with the provisions of ¶¶ 340–352 be paid.

¶ **360.** Effective men who have not been able to obtain their allowance from the people among whom they have labored may present a claim to the Conference, to be paid out of the money at the disposal of the Conference, and such claim may be paid, or any part thereof, as the Conference may determine. In no case, however, shall the Church or Conference be holden accountable for any deficiency, as in the case of debt.

¶ **361.** Every Annual Conference has full liberty to adopt and recommend such plans and rules as to it may appear necessary the more effectually to raise supplies for the respective allowances. Each Annual Conference is authorized to raise a fund, if it judge proper, subject to its own control, and under such regulations as its wisdom may direct, for the relief of the distressed Traveling and Superannuated Preachers, their wives, widows, and children; and it shall be the duty of each Annual Conference to take measures, from year to year, to raise money in every Circuit and Station within its bounds for those purposes.

Building and Renting Houses for the Use of Traveling Preachers.

¶ 362. It is recommended by the General Conference to the Traveling Preachers to advise our friends in general to purchase a lot of ground in each Circuit, and to build a Preacher's house thereon, and to furnish it with, at least, heavy furniture.

¶ 363. The General Conference recommends to all the Circuits, in cases where they are not able to comply with the above request, to rent a house for the married Preacher and his family, (when such are stationed upon their Circuits respectively,) and that the Annual Conferences do assist to make up the rents of such houses as far as they can, when the Circuit cannot do it.

¶ 364. The Stewards in each Circuit and Station shall be a standing Committee (where no Trustees are constituted for that purpose) to provide houses for the families of our married Preachers, or to assist the Preachers to obtain houses for themselves when they are appointed to labor among them.

¶ 365. It shall be the duty of the Presiding Elders and Preachers to use their influence to carry the above rules, respecting building and renting houses for the accommodation of Preachers and their families, into effect. In order to this, each Quarterly Conference shall appoint a Committee, (unless other measures have been adopted,) which, with the advice and aid of the Preachers and Presiding Elders, shall devise such means as may seem fit to raise moneys for that purpose. And it is recommended to the Annual Conferences to make a special inquiry of their members respecting this part of their duty.

PART V.—CHAPTER III.

CHURCHES AND CHURCH PROPERTY.

Building Churches.

¶ 366. Let all our churches be built plain and decent, and with free seats wherever practicable; but not more expensive than is absolutely unavoidable.

¶ 367. In order more effectually to prevent our people from contracting debts which they are not able to discharge, it shall be the duty of the Quarterly Conference of every Circuit and Station where it is contemplated to build a house or houses of worship to secure the ground or lot on which such house or houses are to be built, according to our Deed of Settlement, which deed must be legally executed; and also said Quarterly Conference shall appoint a judicious Committee of at least three members of our Church, who shall form an estimate of the amount necessary to build; and three fourths of the money, according to such estimate, shall be secured or subscribed before any such building shall be commenced.

¶ 368. In all cases where debts for building houses of worship have been, or may be, incurred contrary to or in disregard of the above recommendation, our members and friends are requested to discountenance such a course by declining to give pecuniary aid to all agents who shall travel abroad beyond their own Circuits or Districts for the collection of funds for the discharge of such debts: except in such peculiar cases as may be approved by an Annual Conference, or such agents as may be appointed by their authority.

¶ 369. In future we will admit no charter, deed, or conveyance for any house of worship to be used by us, unless it be provided in such charter, deed, or conveyance that the Trustees of said house shall at all times permit such Ministers and Preachers belonging to the Methodist Episcopal Church as shall from time to time be duly authorized by the General Conference of the Ministers of our Church, or by the Annual Conferences, to preach and expound God's holy word, and to execute the discipline of the Church, and to administer the sacraments therein, according to the true meaning and purport of our Deed of Settlement.

Trustees—Their Appointment, Duties, and Responsibilities.

¶ 370. Each Board of Trustees of our Church property shall consist of not less than three nor more than nine persons, each of whom shall be not less than twenty-one years of age, two thirds of whom shall be members of the Methodist Episcopal Church.

¶ 371. In all cases where the law of the State or Territory requires a specified mode of election, that mode shall be observed.

¶ 372. Where no such specific requirement is made, the Trustees shall be elected annually, by the fourth Quarterly Conference of the Circuit or Station, upon the nomination of the Preacher in Charge, or the Presiding Elder of the District. In case of failure to elect at the proper time a subsequent Quarterly Conference may elect; and all the Trustees shall hold their office until their successors are elected.

¶ 373. All the foregoing provisions shall apply both to the creation of new Boards and to the filling of vacancies, whether for houses of worship or dwellings for the Preachers.

¶ 374. *Provided, nevertheless*, That if the said Trustees, or any of them, or their successors, have advanced, or shall advance, any sum or sums of money, or are or shall be responsible for any sum or sums of money on account of the said premises, and they, the said Trustees, or their successors, be obliged to pay the said sums of money, they, or a majority of them, shall be authorized to raise the said sum or sums of money by a mortgage on the said premises, or by selling the said premises, after notice given to the Pastor or Preacher who has the oversight of the congregation attending Divine service on the said premises, if the money due be not paid to the said Trustees, or their successors, within one year after such notice given: and if such sale take place, the said Trustees, or their successors, after paying the debt and other expenses which are due from the money arising from such sale, shall pay the balance, if not needed and applied for the purchase or improvement of other property for the use of the Church, to the Annual Conference, within whose bounds such property is located; and in case of the re-organization of the said Society, and the erection of a new church building within five years after such transfer of funds, then the said Annual Conference shall repay to said new corporation the moneys which it had received from the Church or Society as above mentioned.

¶ 375. No person who is a Trustee shall be ejected while he is in joint security for money, unless such relief be given him as is demanded, or the creditor will accept, provided he remain a member of our Church.

¶ 376. Charters obtained for our Church property shall conform in the manner of creating and filling Boards of Trustees to the provisions of this chapter.

¶ 377. The Board or Boards of Trustees in any Circuits or Stations shall hold all our Church property, using so much of the proceeds as may be needful to pay debts or to make repairs; and shall be amenable to the Quarterly Conference, to which they shall make an annual report, at the fourth Quarterly Conference, embracing the following items:—1. Number of Churches and Parsonages. 2. Their probable value. 3. Title by which held. 4. Income. 5. Expenditures. 6. Debts, and how contracted. 7. Insurance. 8. Amount raised during the year for building or improving Churches or Parsonages.

Form for Conveyance of Church Property.

¶ 378. In all conveyances of ground for the erection of houses of worship, or upon which they may have been already erected, let the following clause be inserted at the proper place: "In trust that said premises shall be used, kept, maintained, and disposed of as a place of Divine worship for the use of the ministry and membership of the Methodist Episcopal Church in the United States of America; subject to the Discipline, usage, and ministerial appointments of said Church as from time to time authorized and declared by the General Conference of said Church, and the Annual Conference within whose bounds the said premises are situate."

¶ 379. In all conveyances of ground for the erection of dwelling-houses for the use of the Preachers, or upon which they may have been already erected, let the following clause be inserted at the proper place: "In trust that said premises shall be held, kept, and maintained as a place of residence for the use and occupancy of the Preachers of the Methodist Episcopal Church in the United States of America who may, from time to time, be stationed in said place; subject to the usage and Discipline of said Church, as from time to time authorized and declared by the General Conference of said Church, and by the Annual Conference within whose bounds said premises are situate."

¶ **380.** In all other parts of such conveyances, as well as in their attestation, acknowledgment, and placing them upon the record, let a careful conformity be had to the laws, usages, and forms of the several States and Territories in which the property may be situated, so as to secure the ownership of the premises *in fee simple;* and in no case shall the Trustees mortgage or encumber the real estate for the current expenses of the Church.

¶ **381.** Whenever it shall become necessary for the payment of debts, or with a view to reinvestment, to make a sale of Church property that may have been conveyed to Trustees for either of the foregoing purposes, said Trustees or their successors may, upon application to the Quarterly Conference, obtain an order—

a majority of all the members of such Quarterly Conference concurring, and the Preacher in Charge and the Presiding Elder of the District consenting—for the sale, with such limitations and restrictions as said Quarterly Conference may judge necessary; and said Trustees, so authorized, may proceed to sell and convey said property: *provided*, that in all cases the proceeds of the sale, after the payment of debts, if any, if not applied to the purchase or improvement of other property for the same uses, and deeded to the Corporation in the same manner, shall be held by such Corporation subject to the order of the Annual Conference within whose bounds such property is located, or to the Trustees of the Conference fund; and in all cases where Church property is abandoned, or no longer used for the purpose originally designed, it shall be the duty of the Trustees, if any remain, to sell such property and pay over the proceeds to the Annual Conference within whose bounds it is located; and where no such lawful Trustees remain, it shall be the duty of said Annual Conference to secure the custody of such Church property by such means as the laws of the State may afford, subject to be returned in the same manner and upon the same contingencies as named in ¶ 374.

¶ **382.** Houses of worship and dwellings for the use of preachers may be removed from one place to another on the same conditions on which the same may be sold.

Trusteeship.

¶ **383.** There shall be located at Cincinnati an incorporated Board of Trustees of the Methodist Episcopal Church, composed of twelve members, six ministers and six laymen, appointed by the General Conference, of whom three of each class shall hold office four years, and three of each class eight years; all vacancies to be filled quadrennially by the General Conference. The duty of this Board shall be to hold in trust, for the benefit of the Methodist Episcopal Church, any and all donations, bequests, grants, and funds in trust, etc., that may be given or conveyed to said Board, or to the Methodist Episcopal Church, as such, for any benevolent object, and to administer the said funds, and the proceeds of the same, in accordance with the directions of the donors, and of the interests of the Church contemplated by said donors, under the direction of the General Conference: *provided*, That any sums thus donated or bequeathed, but not especially designated for any benevolent object, shall be appropriated to the "Permanent Fund."

¶ **384.** When any such donation, bequest, grant, or trust, etc., is made to this Board, or to the Church, it shall be the duty of the Preacher in the bounds of whose charge it occurs, to give an early notice thereof to the Board, which shall proceed without delay to take possession of the same, according to the provisions of its Charter.

¶ **385.** The Board shall make a faithful report of its doings, and of the funds and property on hand, at each quadrennial session of the General Conference of the Methodist Episcopal Church.

PART V.—CHAPTER IV.

BOUNDARIES OF CONFERENCES.

Mode of Determining Boundaries.

¶ 386. No petition, resolution, or memorial, asking for or involving the division of Conferences, or the organization of new Conferences out of territory already occupied by organized Conferences, or the absorption of Conferences already-existing, shall be entertained by the General Conference until it has first been submitted to the Annual Conferences to be directly affected by such proposed action.

¶ 387. No proposition for any change in Conference boundaries shall be entertained by the General Conference until due notice shall have been given by the Annual Conference desiring such change, or by a majority of the Presiding Elders thereof, to the Conference or Conferences which are to be affected by such proposed action.

¶ 388. Any two or more Conferences which may be mutually interested in the re-adjustment of their common boundaries may at any time raise a joint commission, consisting of five members from each Conference directly interested, and the decision of such joint commission, when it shall be approved by the Bishop or Bishops who may preside in these Conferences at their sessions next ensuing, shall be final. But if the commission so appointed shall fail to agree, or the presiding Bishops shall not concur, then the case, with a statement of its facts, together with the records of the commission, shall come to the General Conference for final adjudication.

¶ 389. The General Conference shall appoint a Committee on Boundaries consisting of one member from each Annual Conference, to be nominated by the delegations severally, over which one of the Bishops shall preside, and of which one of the General Conference Secretaries shall be the Secretary, and of which Committee twenty-five shall be a quorum. All matters pertaining to Conference lines shall be referred to this Committee, and its decision shall be final.

Boundaries of the Annual Conferences.

¶ **390.** (1.) ALABAMA CONFERENCE shall include the Lebanon, Birmingham, West Alabama, and South Alabama Districts, embracing also the Sand Mountain and Scottsborough Charges.

¶ **391.** (2.) ARKANSAS CONFERENCE shall include the State of Arkansas and the Indian country west of the State.

¶ **392.** (3.) BALTIMORE CONFERENCE shall embrace the District of Columbia, the Western Shore of Maryland, excepting so much of Garrett County as lies west of the dividing ridge of the Alleghany Mountains, and including so much of the State of Pennsylvania as lies within the Hancock, Flintstone, Union Grove, and New Bridgeport Circuits, the County of Frederick, the city of Fredericksburgh, in the State of Virginia, and the counties of Jefferson, Berkeley, Morgan, Hampshire, Mineral, Hardy, Pendleton, and Grant, in the State of West Virginia.

¶ **393.** (4.) CALIFORNIA CONFERENCE shall embrace that part of the State of California lying west of the summit of the Sierra Nevada Mountains, and north of a line commencing at the north-west corner of San Luis Obispo County, and extending eastward with the northern line of San Luis Obispo and Tulare Counties: and also the Sandwich Islands.

¶ **394.** (5.) CENTRAL ALABAMA CONFERENCE shall include the Dadesville, Marion, and Huntsville Districts.

¶ **395.** (6.) CENTRAL GERMAN CONFERENCE shall comprise the German work within the States of Ohio, West Virginia, Michigan, and Indiana, except those appointments belonging at present to the Chicago German Conference; also, the German work in the States of Kentucky, Tennessee, and Western Pennsylvania; and shall also include Golconda and Metropolis, Illinois.

¶ **396.** (7.) CENTRAL ILLINOIS CONFERENCE shall embrace that part of the State of Illinois north of the Illinois Conference, and south of the following line, namely: beginning on the Mississippi River at the Meredosia; thence down the Meredosia to its mouth; thence easterly to Center School-House, so as to include Center Society; thence to the mouth of Mud Creek; thence up Green River to Coal Creek; thence up said creek to the Chicago and Rock Island Railroad;

thence along said railroad to Bureau Junction; thence to the Illinois River; thence up said river and the Kankakee to the Indiana State line, leaving the city of Ottawa in the Rock River Conference, and Aroma and Bureau Junction in the Central Illinois Conference.

¶ 397. (8.) CENTRAL NEW YORK CONFERENCE shall be bounded on the west by the East Genesee Conference, on the south by the New York State line and the Wyoming Conference, and on the east and north by the Wyoming and the Northern New York Conferences.

¶ 398. (9.) CENTRAL OHIO CONFERENCE shall be bounded on the north by the north line of the State of Ohio; on the east by the North Ohio Conference; on the south by the Springfield branch of the Cleveland, Columbus, and Cincinnati Railroad to the west line of the Ohio Conference, yet so as to exclude St. Paul's Charge in Delaware, and Milford, and to include Marysville; thence to the west line of the State of Ohio, by the north line of the Cincinnati Conference; and on the west by the west line of the State of Ohio.

¶ 399. (10.) CENTRAL PENNSYLVANIA

CONFERENCE shall be bounded as follows: On the south by the State line from the Susquehanna River to the west boundary of Bedford County, excepting so much of the State of Pennsylvania as is included in the Baltimore Conference; on the west by the west line of Bedford, Blair, and Clearfield Counties, except so much of Clearfield County as is embraced in the Erie Conference; thence to St. Mary's; on the north by a line extending from St. Mary's eastward to Emporium; thence by the southern boundary of Potter and Tioga Counties, including Wharton, and Liberty Valley Circuit; thence through Sullivan County north of Laporte, to the west line of Wyoming County; on the east by Wyoming Conference to the north line of the Philadelphia Conference; thence on the northern line of Carbon, Schuylkill, and Dauphin Counties to the Susquehanna River, including Hickory Run, Weatherly, Beaver Meadow, and Ashland; and thence by the Susquehanna River to the place of beginning, including Harrisburgh.

¶ 400. (11.) CHICAGO GERMAN CONFERENCE shall include all the State of Wisconsin, except those appointments along the Mississippi River and that part of the State of Illinois north of an east and west line passing along the north line of the City of Bloomington, (also excepting the territory now in the South-west German Conference,) and east of a north and south line passing through the city of Freeport and that part of the State of Indiana west of the line between the Counties of St. Joseph and Elkhart, and north of the line between Stark and Pulaski Counties. It shall also include Danville, Illinois.

¶ **401.** (12.) CINCINNATI CONFERENCE shall be bounded on the north by a line commencing at the south-west corner of Darke County in the State of Ohio; thence easterly to the north-west corner of the Ohio Conference, so as to leave Bellefontaine and Delaware Districts in the Central Ohio Conference; on the east by the Ohio Conference; on the south by the Ohio River; and on the west by the State of Indiana, except so much of a variation of that line as to attach Elizabeth, Hamilton County, Ohio, to the South-eastern Indiana Conference.

¶ **402.** (13.) COLORADO CONFERENCE shall include Colorado Territory and that part of the Territory of Wyoming lying north of Colorado.

¶ **403.** (14.) COLUMBIA RIVER CONFERENCE shall include all of the State of Oregon lying east of the Cascade Mountains, except Lake County; all of Washington Territory lying east of the Cascade Mountains, and all of Idaho Territory lying directly north of the State of Nevada.

¶ **404.** (15.) DELAWARE CONFERENCE shall include the territory east and north of the Washington Conference.

¶ **405.** (16.) DES MOINES CONFERENCE shall include that part of the State of Iowa west and south of the following lines: Beginning at the south-east corner of Wayne County; thence north to the south line of Marshall County, (leaving Knoxville to the Iowa Conference, and Monroe to the Des Moines Conference;) thence west to the south-east corner of Story County; thence north to the north-east corner of Story County; thence west to the north-east corner of Crawford County; thence south to the north line of township eighty-three; thence west to the east line of Monona County; thence south and west on the line of Monona County to the Missouri River.

¶ **406.** (17.) DETROIT CONFERENCE shall include that part of the State of Michigan east of the principal meridian, and also the Upper Peninsula.

¶ **407.** (18.) EAST GENESEE CONFERENCE shall be bounded on the west by the Genesee River, including the city of Rochester, in the State of New York, on the north by Lake Ontario, on the east by a line beginning at Sodus Bay and running south on the east line of the towns of Sodus and Lyons in Wayne County, and the east line of Ontario County to Seneca Lake, thence southward up said lake to Watkins, thence south to the New York State line, leaving the charges of Watkins, Havana, Millport, and Horseheads in Central New York Conference. It shall also include the territory in the State of Pennsylvania known as the Troy District.

¶ **408.** (19.) EAST GERMAN CONFERENCE shall embrace the German work east of the Alleghany Mountains.

¶ **409.** (20.) EAST MAINE CONFERENCE shall include that part of the State of Maine not included in the Maine Conference.

¶ **410.** (21.) EAST OHIO CONFERENCE

shall be bounded by a line beginning at the mouth of the Cuyahoga River, and running easterly to the Pennsylvania State line; thence along said line leaving the Petersburgh Society in the Erie Conference, to the Ohio River; thence down said river to the Muskingum River; thence up said river to the Ohio Canal near Dresden, excluding Marietta and Zanesville; thence along said canal to Lake Erie, including Akron and all of the city of Cleveland lying east of the Cuyahoga River.

¶ 411. (22.) ERIE CONFERENCE shall be bounded on the north by Lake Erie, on the east by a line commencing at the mouth of the Cattaraugus Creek; thence up said creek to the village of Gowanda, leaving said village in the Western New York Conference; thence to the Alleghany River at the mouth of the Tunungwant Creek; thence up said creek southward to the ridge dividing between the waters of Clarion and Sinnemahoning Creeks; thence southward to the Mahoning Creek; thence down said creek, exclusive of the Milton Society, but including Finley Society, in the Punxutawney Circuit, and Putneyville in the Bethlehem Circuit, to the Alleghany River; thence across said river in a north-westerly direction to the Western Reserve line, including Wampum and Petersburgh; thence along the State line to the place of beginning, including Orangeville and the State line appointments on the Jamestown Circuit.

¶ **412.** (23.) FLORIDA CONFERENCE shall include the State of Florida.

¶ **413.** (24.) FOOCHOW CONFERENCE shall include the Fokien Province in China.

¶ **414.** (25.) GEORGIA CONFERENCE shall consist of the Atlanta, Dalton, and Ogeechee Districts.

¶ **415.** (26.) GERMANY AND SWITZERLAND CONFERENCE shall include the work in Germany and those portions of France and Switzerland where the German language is spoken.

¶ **416.** (27.) HOLSTON CONFERENCE shall be bounded on the east by Virginia; on the north by Virginia and Kentucky; on the west by the western summit of the Cumberland Mountains; on the south by Georgia and the Blue Ridge, including that portion of North Carolina not within the North Carolina Conference.

¶ **417.** (28.) ILLINOIS CONFERENCE shall include that part of the State of Illinois not within the Southern Illinois Conference, south of the following line, namely: Beginning at Warsaw on the Mississippi River; thence to Vermont; thence to the mouth of the Spoon River; thence up the Illinois River to the north-west corner of Mason County; thence to the junction of the Central and the Alton and Chicago Railroads; thence to the south-west corner of Iroquois County; thence east to the State of Indiana, leaving Bentley, Vermont, Mackinaw Circuit, and Normal in the Central Illinois, and Warsaw and Bloomington in the Illinois Conference.

¶ **418.** (29.) INDIANA CONFERENCE shall be bounded on the north and east by a line beginning where the National Road intersects the west line of the State of Indiana; thence along said road to Terre Haute; thence along the St. Louis, Vandalia, Terre Haute, and Indianapolis Railroad to the corporation line of Indianapolis; thence north and east by said corporation line to the Michigan Road; thence south by said road to the Indianapolis and Lafayette Railroad;

thence south by said railroad to Third-street; thence east by Third-street to Meridian-street; thence south by Meridian-street, Madison Avenue, and Madison Pike to the southern limits of the city; thence west to White River; thence down said river to the west line of Johnson County, thence south on the west line of Johnson, Brown, Jackson, Scott, and Clarke Counties to the Ohio River; on the south by the Ohio River; and on the west by the State of Illinois.

¶ 419. (30.) IOWA CONFERENCE shall be bounded on the east by the Mississippi River; on the south by the Missouri State line; on the west and north by a line commencing at the south-west corner of Appanoose County; thence north to Marshall County, leaving Knoxville in the Iowa Conference and Monroe in the Des Moines Conference; thence on the south line of Marshall County due east to Iowa River; thence down said river to Iowa City; thence on the Chicago, Rock Island, and Pacific Railroad to Davenport, leaving Davenport and Iowa City in the Upper Iowa Conference, and all intermediate towns in the Iowa Conference.

¶ **420.** (31.) KANSAS CONFERENCE shall embrace that portion of the State of Kansas lying north of the south line of township sixteen, including the town of Pomona, which lies south of said line, but shall leave Louisburgh, Ottawa, and Baldwin City, lying north of said line, in the South Kansas Conference. Baldwin City shall belong to South Kansas Conference after the session of said Conference in 1877.

¶ **421.** (32.) KENTUCKY CONFERENCE shall include the State of Kentucky.

¶ **422.** (33.) LEXINGTON CONFERENCE shall include the States of Kentucky, Ohio, Indiana, and Illinois.

¶ **423.** (34.) LIBERIA CONFERENCE shall embrace the western coast of Africa.

¶ **424.** (35.) LOUISIANA CONFERENCE shall include the State of Louisiana.

¶ **425.** (36.) MAINE CONFERENCE shall include that part of the State of Maine west of the Kennebec River from its mouth to the great bend below Skowhegan, and of a line running thence north to the State line, including Skowhegan and Augusta, and also that part of New Hampshire east of the White Hills, and north of the waters of Ossipee Lake and the town of Gorham.

¶ **426.** (37.) MICHIGAN CONFERENCE shall include the State of Michigan west of the principal meridian in the Lower Peninsula.

¶ **427.** (38.) MINNESOTA CONFERENCE shall include the State of Minnesota.

¶ **428.** (39.) MISSISSIPPI CONFERENCE shall include the State of Mississippi.

¶ **429.** (40.) MISSOURI CONFERENCE shall include so much of the State of Missouri as lies north of the Missouri River.

¶ **430.** (41.) NEBRASKA CONFERENCE shall embrace the State of Nebraska.

¶ **431.** (42.) NEVADA CONFERENCE shall include Nevada and so much of California as lies east of the west summit of the Sierra Nevada Mountains.

¶ **432.** (43.) NEWARK CONFERENCE shall include that part of the State of New Jersey not included in the New Jersey Conference, Staten Island, and so much of New York and Pennsylvania as lies within the Jersey City and Newton Districts.

¶ **433.** (44.) NEW ENGLAND CONFERENCE shall include all of Massachusetts east of the Green Mountains not included in the New Hampshire and Providence Conferences.

¶ **434.** (45.) NEW HAMPSHIRE CONFERENCE shall include New Hampshire, except that part within the Maine Conference; also that part of Massachusetts north-east of the Merrimac River.

¶ **435.** (46.) NEW JERSEY CONFERENCE shall include that part of New Jersey south of the following line, namely: Commencing at Raritan Bay; thence up said bay and river to New Brunswick; thence along the turnpike road to Lambertville on the Delaware, including the city of New Brunswick and Lambertville Station.

¶ **436.** (47.) NEW YORK CONFERENCE shall consist of the territory now in the New York, Poughkeepsie, (including Gaylordsville,) Newburgh, Prattsville, and Ellenville Districts.

¶ **437.** (48.) NEW YORK EAST CONFERENCE shall include the New York, Bridgeport, New Haven, and the two Long Island Districts, including those Charges in the city of New York east of a line running through Third Avenue, Bowery, Chatham-street, Park Row, and Broadway.

¶ **438.** (49.) NORTH CAROLINA CONFERENCE shall include the State of North Carolina, excepting the counties west of Wautauga County, and the Blue Ridge, now included in the Holston Conference.

¶ **439.** (50.) NORTHERN NEW YORK CONFERENCE shall include so much of the County of Franklin as is not within the Troy Conference, and all of the Counties of St. Lawrence, Jefferson, Lewis, Oneida, and Herkimer, and all of Oswego County except Phenix, and so much of the County of Madison as lies on and east of the New York and Midland Railroad, together with Cherry Valley, Springfield, and Richfield Springs in Otsego County, Sharon Springs in Schoharie County, and Frey's Bush, Ames, and St. Johnsville in Montgomery County.

¶ **440.** (51.) NORTH INDIA CONFERENCE shall include the Province of Oudh and the Districts of Rohilcund, Cawnpore, Kumaon, and Gurhwal in the North-west Province.

¶ **441.** (52.) NORTH INDIANA CONFERENCE shall be bounded on the north by Michigan; on the east by Ohio, including Union City; on the south by the National Road, from the State line west to Marion

County, thence north to the north-east corner of said county, thence west to the Michigan Road; on the west by said Michigan Road to South Bend, and thence by the St. Joseph River to the Michigan State line, including Logansport and all towns on the National Road east of Indianapolis.

¶ **442.** (53.) NORTH OHIO CONFERENCE shall be bounded on the north by the Ohio State line; on the east by East Ohio Conference, and Tuscarawas and Muskingum Rivers, to Dresden; on the south by Ohio Conference, including Utica, Homer, and Galena Circuits, and excluding Stratford; on the west by the main road passing through Delaware and Marion to Upper Sandusky, and the Sandusky River, excluding so much of the town of Delaware as lies west of the Olentangy River, and also excluding the towns of Marion, Fremont, and Upper Sandusky, and including Tiffin.

¶ **443.** (54.) NORTH-WEST GERMAN CONFERENCE shall include the State of Minnesota and that part of the State of Iowa north of an east and west line passing along the south line of the city of Clinton, and that part of the State of

Illinois lying west of the bounds of the Chicago German Conference.

¶ **444.** (55.) NORTH-WEST INDIANA CONFERENCE shall be bounded on the north by Lake Michigan and the State line; on the east by the St. Joseph River and the Michigan Road; on the south by the Indiana Conference; and on the west by Illinois, including all the towns on the Michigan Road except Logansport and Plainfield, and all the towns on the southern boundary.

¶ **445.** (56.) NORTH-WEST IOWA CONFERENCE shall include that part of the State of Iowa west of the Upper Iowa and north of the Des Moines Conferences, and shall also include Dakota Territory.

¶ **446.** (57.) NORWAY CONFERENCE shall embrace Norway in Europe.

¶ **447.** (58.) OHIO CONFERENCE shall be bounded as follows: Commencing on the Muskingum River south of Dresden; thence down said River to the Ohio River, including Zanesville and Marietta; thence down the Ohio River to the mouth of Ohio Brush Creek; thence north to the south-east corner of Fayette County; thence north-west to the west line of Fayette County; thence north on the west line of the Fayette and Madison Counties to the Springfield branch of the Cleveland, Columbus, and Cincinnati Railroad leaving Vienna, Dunbarton, and Sinking Springs Circuits west of said line; thence east on the southern boundaries of Central Ohio and North Ohio Conferences to place of beginning, including Milford, Stratford, and St. Paul's Charge in Delaware.

¶ 448. (59.) OREGON CONFERENCE shall include that part of the State of Oregon and Washington Territory lying west of the Cascade Mountains, and so much of what is known as Goose Lake Valley as lies within the State of Oregon.

¶ **449.** (60.) PHILADELPHIA CONFERENCE shall be bounded on the east by the Delaware River; on the south by the Pennsylvania State line; on the west by the Susquehanna River, excluding Harrisburgh; on the north by the north lines of Dauphin, Schuylkill, Carbon, and Monroe Counties, excepting Ashland and Beaver Meadows Circuit.

¶ **450.** (61.) PITTSBURGH CONFERENCE shall be bounded on the north by Erie Conference; on the east by the summit of the Alleghany Mountains to the southern boundary of Pennsylvania, excluding

New Washington Circuit; thence west along the line of the West Virginia Conference to the Ohio River; thence up said river to the Pennsylvania State line, thence along said line to the Erie Conference.

¶ **452.** (62.) PROVIDENCE CONFERENCE shall include that part of Connecticut east of Connecticut River; the State of Rhode Island, with Millville and Blackstone in Massachusetts; and also that part of Massachusetts south-east of a line drawn from the north-east corner of Rhode Island to the mouth of Neponset River, leaving Walpole Station, Foxborough, and Quincy Point in the New England Conference.

¶ **453.** (63.) ROCK RIVER CONFERENCE shall include that part of Illinois north of the Central Illinois Conference.

¶ **454.** (64.) ROCKY MOUNTAIN CONFERENCE shall include the Territories of Utah, Montana, and Idaho, excepting so much as lies directly north of Nevada, and that portion of Wyoming Territory not included in the Colorado Conference.

¶ **455.** (65.) SAINT LOUIS CONFERENCE shall include the State of Missouri lying south of Missouri River.

¶ **456.** (66.) SAVANNAH CONFERENCE shall consist of the Rome, Macon, Augusta, and Savannah Districts.

¶ **457.** (67.) SOUTH CAROLINA CONFERENCE shall include the State of South Carolina.

¶ **458.** (68.) SOUTH-EAST INDIANA CONFERENCE shall be bounded as follows, namely: Beginning at the crossing of Meridian and Third streets, in the city of Indianapolis; thence west by said Third-street to the Indianapolis and Lafayette Railroad; thence north on said railroad to the Michigan Road; thence on said road to the north line of Marion County; thence east on said county line to the north-east corner of said county; thence south on the east line of said county to the National Road; thence east on said Road to the State line; on the east by Ohio, so as to include Elizabeth, Hamilton County, Ohio; on the south by the Ohio River; and on the west by the Indiana Conference.

¶ **459.** (69.) SOUTHERN CALIFORNIA CONFERENCE shall embrace that portion of the State of California lying south of the California Conference; also that portion of the State east of the summit of the Sierra Nevada Mountains, and south of Inyo County.

¶ **460.** (70.) SOUTHERN GERMAN CONFERENCE shall include the State of Texas.

¶ **461.** (71.) SOUTHERN ILLINOIS CONFERENCE shall include that part of the State of Illinois south of the following line, namely: Beginning at the mouth of Illinois River; thence up said river to the north-west corner of Jersey County, including Kane and Woodbury; thence to Honey Point; thence to Hillsborough, leaving it in the Illinois Conference; thence east through Fayette and Effingham Counties to the north-east corner of Jasper County; thence on the north line of Jasper and Crawford Counties to the Wabash River.

¶ **462.** (72.) SOUTH INDIA CONFERENCE shall include all those parts of India not embraced in the North India Conference.

¶ **463.** (73.) SOUTH KANSAS CONFERENCE shall embrace that portion of the State of Kansas not included in the Kansas Conference, and so much of the Indian Territory south thereof as lies north of the thirty-sixth parallel of north latitude.

¶ **464.** (74.) SOUTH-WEST GERMAN

CONFERENCE shall comprise the German work formerly connected with Illinois, Southern Illinois, and Kansas Conferences, and the German District of the Upper Iowa Conference.

¶ **465.** (75.) SWEDEN CONFERENCE shall embrace Sweden in Europe.

¶ **466.** (76.) TENNESSEE CONFERENCE shall include that portion of Tennessee not included in the Holston Conference.

¶ **467.** (77.) TEXAS CONFERENCE shall include so much of the State of Texas as lies east of a line beginning at the Gulf of Mexico on the east line of Matagorda County, and running along said line and the east line of Wharton and Colorado Counties, to the north point of Colorado County, thence north until it strikes the Central Railroad at Calvert; thence along the line of said railroad to the northern boundary of Texas, excluding Calvert, and all the towns on the line of said road.

¶ **468.** (78.) TROY CONFERENCE shall include Troy, Albany, Saratoga, Plattsburgh, and Cambridge Districts, and Burlington District in Vermont.

¶ **469.** (79.) UPPER IOWA CONFERENCE shall be bounded as follows, to wit: Beginning at the north-east corner of the State of Iowa; thence down the Mississippi River to Davenport; thence west on the north line of the Iowa Conference to the south-east corner of Story County; thence north to the State line so as to include Iowa Falls; thence east on said line to the place of beginning.

¶ 470. (80.) VERMONT CONFERENCE shall include the State of Vermont, excepting that part within the Troy Conference.

¶ 471. (81.) VIRGINIA CONFERENCE shall include all the State of Virginia not embraced in the Baltimore and Wilmington Conferences, and also the counties of Pocahontas, Green Brier, and Monroe in the State of West Virginia.

¶ 472. (82.) WASHINGTON CONFERENCE shall include Western Maryland, the District of Columbia, Virginia, West Virginia, and so much of the State of Pennsylvania as lies west of the Susquehanna River, including the towns on said river.

¶ 473. (83.) WESTERN NEW YORK CONFERENCE shall include all that part of the State of New York lying west of the East Genesee Conference, excepting that part of Cattaraugus and Chautauqua Counties now included in the Erie Conference, together with so much of Potter County, in the State of Pennsylvania, as is not included in the Central Pennsylvania Conference, leaving Brookfield and Gaines Charges in the East Genesee Conference, and including so much of McKean County as is embraced in the Olean District.

¶ 474. (84.) WEST TEXAS CONFERENCE shall embrace so much of the State of Texas as is not included in the Texas Conference.

¶ 475. (85.) WEST VIRGINIA CONFERENCE shall be bounded as follows: Beginning at the south-west corner of the State of Pennsylvania; thence along said line to the north-east corner of Ohio County, West Virginia, so as to include Wheeling Creek Mission and Triadelphia Circuit; thence the most direct way to Short Creek, so as to include Short Creek and Liberty Circuit; thence down said creek to the Ohio River; thence down said river to the mouth of the Big Sandy River; on the west by the State line; on the south and east by the Virginia and Baltimore Conferences, to the Pennsylvania State line; thence westward along said line to the place of beginning.

¶ 476. (86.) WEST WISCONSIN CONFERENCE shall include that part of the State of Wisconsin not embraced in the Wisconsin Conference.

¶ 477. (87.) WILMINGTON CONFERENCE shall include the State of Delaware and the Eastern Shores of Maryland and Virginia.

¶ 478. (88.) WISCONSIN CONFERENCE shall include all that part of the State of Wisconsin lying east and north of a line beginning at the south-east corner of Greene County, on the south line of the State; thence north on the range line between ranges nine (9) and ten (10) east, to the north line of town twenty (20); thence west on the said line to the east line of range one (1) east; thence north on said line to the north line of town forty (40); thence west on said line to the State line on the west.

¶ 479. (89.) WYOMING CONFERENCE shall include the southern part of the State of New York not included in the New York, New York East, Newark, Central New York, and Western New York Conferences, and that part of Pennsylvania bounded on the west by Central New York Conference, including the territory east of the Susquehanna, and on the south by the Central Pennsylvania, Philadelphia, and Newark Conferences, including Narrowsburgh, and on the east by the Newark and New York Conferences.

¶ **480.** SCANDINAVIAN WORK.

§ 1. The Swedish and Norwegian work within the Minnesota, West Wisconsin, Upper Iowa, and North-west Iowa Conferences shall belong to the Minnesota Conference.

§ 2. The Swedish work within the bounds of the Iowa, Central Illinois, Rock River, and Wisconsin Conferences shall belong to the Central Illinois Conference.

§ 3. The Norwegian work within the bounds of the Wisconsin and Rock River Conferences shall belong to the Wisconsin Conference.

§ 4. The Swedish and Norwegian work in the cities of New York and Brooklyn, and in the vicinity of those cities, shall belong to the New York East Conference.

PART VI.

THE RITUAL.

Order of Baptism.

¶ 481. THE MINISTRATION OF BAPTISM TO INFANTS.

The Minister, coming to the Font, which is to be filled with pure Water, shall use the following:—

DEARLY BELOVED: Forasmuch as all men are conceived and born in sin, and that our Saviour Christ saith, Except a man be born of water and of the Spirit he cannot enter into the kingdom of God; I beseech you to call upon God the Father, through our Lord Jesus Christ, that having, of his bounteous mercy, redeemed *this child* by the blood of his Son, he will grant that *he*, being baptized with water, may also be baptized with the Holy Ghost, be received into Christ's holy Church, and become *a lively member* of the same.

Then shall the Minister say,

Let us pray.

Almighty and everlasting God, who of thy great mercy hast condescended to enter into covenant relations with man, wherein thou hast included children as partakers of its gracious benefits, declaring that of such is thy kingdom: and in thy ancient Church didst appoint divers baptisms, figuring thereby the renewing of the Holy Ghost; and by thy well-beloved Son Jesus Christ gavest commandment to thy holy Apostles to go into all the world and disciple all nations, baptizing them in the name of the Father, and of the Son, and of the Holy Ghost: We beseech thee, that of thine infinite mercy thou wilt look upon *this child:* wash *him* and sanctify *him;* that *he*, being saved by thy grace, may be received into Christ's holy Church, and being steadfast in faith, joyful through hope, and rooted in love, may so overcome the evils of this present world, that finally *he* may attain to everlasting life, and reign with thee, world without end, through Jesus Christ our Lord. *Amen.*

O merciful God, grant that all carnal affections may die in *him*, and that all things belonging to the Spirit may live and grow in *him*. *Amen.*

Grant that *he* may have power and strength to have victory, and to triumph against the devil, the world, and the flesh. *Amen.*

Grant that whosoever is dedicated to thee by our office and ministry may also be endued with heavenly virtues, and everlastingly rewarded through thy mercy, O blessed Lord God, who dost live, and govern all things, world without end. *Amen.*

Almighty, ever-living God, whose most dearly beloved Son Jesus Christ, for the forgiveness of our sins, did shed out of his most precious side both water and blood, regard, we beseech thee, our supplications. Sanctify this water for this holy sacrament; and grant that *this child*, now to be baptized, may receive the fullness of thy grace, and ever remain in the number of thy faithful and elect children, through Jesus Christ our Lord. *Amen.*

Then shall the Minister address the Parents [or Guardians] as follows:—

Dearly beloved: Forasmuch as *this child is* now presented by you for Christian baptism, *you* must remember that it is your part and duty to see that *he* be taught, as soon as *he* shall be able to learn, the nature and end of this holy sacrament. And that *he* may know these things the better, *you* shall call upon *him* to give reverent attendance upon the appointed means of grace, such as the ministry of the word and the public and private worship of God; and further, ye shall provide that *he* shall read the Holy Scriptures, and learn the Lord's Prayer, the Ten Commandments, the Apostles' Creed, the Catechism, and all other things which a Christian ought to know and believe to *his* soul's health, in order that *he* may be brought up to lead a virtuous and holy life, remembering always that baptism doth represent unto us that inward purity which disposeth us to follow the example of our Saviour Christ; that as he died and rose again for us, so should we, who are baptized, die unto sin and rise again unto righteousness, continually mortifying all corrupt affections and daily proceeding in all virtue and godliness.

Do *you* therefore solemnly engage to fulfill these duties, so far as in you lies, the Lord being your helper?

Ans. We do.

Then shall the people stand up, and the Minister shall say:—

Hear the words of the Gospel, written by St. Mark. [Chap. x, 13–16.]

They brought young children to Christ, that he should touch them. And his disciples rebuked those that brought them. But when Jesus saw it, he was much displeased, and said unto them, Suffer the little children to come unto me, and forbid them not, for of such is the kingdom of God. Verily I say unto you, Whosoever shall not receive the kingdom of God as a little child, he shall not enter therein. And he took them up in his arms, put his hands upon them, and blessed them.

Then the Minister shall take the Child into his hands, and say to the friends of the Child,

Name this child.

And then, naming it after them, he shall sprinkle or pour Water upon it, or, if desired, immerse it in Water, saying,—

N., I baptize thee in the name of the Father, and of the Son, and of the Holy Ghost. *Amen.*

Then shall the Minister offer the following prayer, the people kneeling:—

O God of infinite mercy, the Father of all the faithful seed, be pleased to grant unto this child an understanding mind and a sanctified heart. May thy providence lead *him* through the dangers, temptations, and ignorance of *his* youth, that *he* may never run into folly nor into the evils of an unbridled appetite. We pray thee so to order the course of *his* life, that by good education, by holy examples, and by thy restraining and renewing grace, *he* may be led to serve thee faithfully all *his* days, so that, when *he* has glorified thee in *his* generation, and has served the Church on earth, *he* may be received into thine eternal kingdom, through Jesus Christ our Lord. *Amen.*

Almighty and most merciful Father, let thy loving mercy and compassion descend upon these, thy servant and handmaid, the parents [or guardians] of this child. Grant unto them, we beseech thee, thy holy Spirit, that they may, like Abraham, command their household to keep the way of the Lord. Direct their actions, and sanctify their hearts, words, and purposes, that their whole family may be united to our Lord Jesus Christ in the bands of faith, obedience, and charity; and that they all, being in this life thy holy children by adoption and grace, may be admitted into the Church of the first-born in heaven, through the merits of thy dear Son, our Saviour and Redeemer. *Amen.*

Then may the Minister offer extemporary prayer.

Then shall be said, all kneeling:—

Our Father who art in heaven, hallowed be thy name. Thy kingdom come. Thy will be done in earth, as it is in heaven. Give us this day our daily bread; and forgive us our trespasses, as we forgive them that trespass against us; and lead us not into temptation, but deliver us from evil; for thine is the kingdom, and the power, and the glory, forever. *Amen.*

¶ 482. THE MINISTRATION OF BAPTISM TO SUCH AS ARE OF RIPER YEARS.

DEARLY BELOVED: Forasmuch as all men are conceived and born in sin; and that which is born of the flesh is flesh, and they that are in the flesh cannot please God, but live in sin, committing many actual transgressions; and our Saviour Christ saith, Except a man be born of water and of the Spirit he cannot enter into the kingdom of God:—I beseech you to call upon God the Father, through our Lord Jesus Christ, that of his bounteous goodness he will grant to *these persons* that which by nature *they* cannot have; that *they*, being baptized with water, may also be baptized with the Holy Ghost, and being received into Christ's holy Church, may continue lively *members* of the same.

Then shall the Minister say,—

Let us pray.

Almighty and immortal God, the aid of all that need, the helper of all that flee to thee for succor, the life of them that believe, and the resurrection of the dead: we call upon thee for *these persons;* that *they*, coming to thy holy baptism, may also be filled with thy Holy Spirit. Receive *them*, O Lord, as thou hast promised by thy well-beloved Son, saying, Ask, and ye shall receive; seek, and ye shall find; knock, and it shall be opened unto you: so give now unto us that ask: let us that seek, find: open the gate unto us that knock; that *these persons* may enjoy the everlasting benediction of thy heavenly washing, and may come to the eternal kingdom which thou hast promised by Christ our Lord. *Amen.*

Then shall the people stand up, and the Minister shall say:—

Hear the words of the Gospel, written by St. John. [Chap. iii, 1-8.]

There was a man of the Pharisees, named Nicodemus, a ruler of the Jews: the same came to Jesus by night, and said unto him, Rabbi, we know that thou art a teacher come from God; for no man can do these miracles that thou doest except God be with him. Jesus answered and said unto him, Verily, verily, I say unto thee, Except a man be born again, he cannot see the kingdom of God. Nicodemus saith unto him, How can a man be born when he is old? Can he enter the second time into his mother's womb, and be born? Jesus answered, Verily, verily, I say unto thee, Except a man be born of water and of the Spirit he cannot enter into the kingdom of God. That which is born of the flesh is flesh, and that which is born of the Spirit is spirit. Marvel not that I said unto thee, Ye must be born again. The wind bloweth where it listeth, and thou hearest the sound thereof but canst not tell whence it cometh, and whither it goeth: so is every one that is born of the Spirit.

Then the Minister shall speak to the persons to be baptized on this wise:—

Well beloved, who *have* come hither desiring to receive holy baptism, you have heard how the congregation hath prayed that our Lord Jesus Christ would vouchsafe to receive you, to bless you, and to give you the kingdom of heaven, and everlasting life. And our Lord Jesus Christ hath promised in his holy word to grant all those things that we have prayed for:

which promise he for his part will most surely keep and perform.

Wherefore after this promise made by Christ, *you* must also faithfully, for *your* part, promise in the presence of this whole congregation, that you will renounce the devil and all his works, and constantly believe God's holy word, and obediently keep his commandments.

Then shall the Minister demand of each of the persons to be baptized:—

Quest. Dost thou renounce the devil and all his works, the vain pomp and glory of the world, with all covetous desires of the same, and the carnal desires of the flesh, so that thou wilt not follow nor be led by them?

Answ. I renounce them all.

Quest. Dost thou believe in God the Father Almighty, Maker of heaven and earth? and in Jesus Christ his only-begotten Son our Lord? and that he was conceived by the Holy Ghost, born of the Virgin Mary? that he suffered under Pontius Pilate, was crucified, dead and buried? that he rose again the third day? that he ascended into heaven, and sitteth at the right hand of God the Father Almighty, and from thence shall come again at the end of the world, to judge the quick and the dead?

And dost thou believe in the Holy Ghost? the holy catholic Church?* the communion of saints? the remission of sins? the resurrection of the body, and everlasting life after death?

Answ. All this I steadfastly believe.

Quest. Wilt thou be baptized in this faith?

Answ. This is my desire.

Quest. Wilt thou then obediently keep God's holy will and commandments, and walk in the same all the days of thy life?

Answ. I will endeavor so to do, God being my helper.

Then shall the Minister say:—

O merciful God, grant that all carnal affections may die in *these persons*, and that all things belonging to the Spirit may live and grow in *them*. *Amen.*

Grant that *they* may have power and strength to have victory, and triumph against the devil, the world, and the flesh. *Amen.*

Grant that *they*, being here dedicated

* The one universal Church of Christ.

to thee by our office and ministry, may also be endued with heavenly virtues, and everlastingly rewarded, through thy mercy, O blessed Lord God, who dost live, and govern all things, world without end. *Amen.*

Almighty, ever-living God, whose most dearly beloved Son Jesus Christ, for the forgiveness of our sins, did shed out of his most precious side both water and blood; and gave commandment to his disciples, that they should go teach all nations, and baptize them in the name of the Father, and of the Son, and of the Holy Ghost; regard, we beseech thee, our supplications; and grant that the *persons* now to be baptized may receive the fullness of thy grace, and ever remain in the number of thy faithful and elect children, through Jesus Christ our Lord. *Amen.*

Then shall the Minister ask the name of each person to be baptized: and shall sprinkle or pour water upon him, (or, if he shall desire it, shall immerse him in water,) saying:—

N., I baptize thee in the name of the Father, and of the Son, and of the Holy Ghost. *Amen.*

Then shall be said the Lord's Prayer, all kneeling.

Our Father who art in heaven, hallowed be thy name. Thy kingdom come. Thy will be done in earth, as it is in heaven. Give us this day our daily bread; and forgive us our trespasses, as we forgive them that trespass against us; and lead us not into temptation, but deliver us from evil; for thine is the kingdom, and the power, and the glory, forever. *Amen.*

Then may the Minister conclude with extemporary prayer.

Reception of Members.

¶ 483. FORM FOR RECEIVING PERSONS INTO THE CHURCH AFTER PROBATION.

Upon the day appointed, all that are to be received shall be called forward, and the Minister, addressing the congregation, shall say:—

DEARLY BELOVED BRETHREN: The Scriptures teach us that the Church is the household of God, the body of which Christ is the Head, and that it is the design of the Gospel to bring together in one all who are in Christ. The fellowship of the Church is the communion that its members enjoy one with another. The ends of this fellowship are, the maintenance of sound doctrine, and of the ordinances of Christian worship, and the exercise of that power of godly admonition and discipline which Christ has committed to his Church for the promotion of holiness. It is the duty of all men to unite in this fellowship, for it is only those that "be planted in the house of the Lord, that shall flourish in the courts of our God." Its more particular *duties* are, to promote peace and unity; to bear one another's burdens; to prevent each other's stumbling; to seek the intimacy of friendly society among themselves; to continue steadfast in the faith and worship of the Gospel; and to pray and sympathize with each other. Among its *privileges* are, peculiar incitements to holiness from the hearing of God's word and sharing in Christ's ordinances; the being placed under the watchful care of pastors, and the enjoyment of the blessings which are promised only to those who are of the household of faith. Into this holy fellowship the persons before you, who have already received the sacrament of baptism, and have been under the care of proper leaders for six months on trial, come seeking admission. We now propose, in the fear of God, to question them as to their faith and purposes, that you may know that they are proper persons to be admitted into the Church.

Then addressing the applicants for admission, the Minister shall say:—

Dearly beloved: You are come hither seeking the great privilege of union with the Church our Saviour has purchased with his own blood. We rejoice in the grace of God vouchsafed unto you in that he has called you to be his *followers*, and that thus far you have run well. You have heard how blessed are the privileges, and how solemn are the duties, of membership in Christ's Church; and before you are fully admitted thereto, it is proper that you do here publicly renew your vows, confess your faith, and declare your purpose, by answering the following questions:—

Do you here, in the presence of God and of this congregation, renew the solemn promise contained in the baptismal covenant, ratifying and confirming the same, and acknowledging yourselves bound faithfully to observe and keep that covenant?

Answ. I do.

Have you saving faith in the Lord Jesus Christ?

Answ. I trust I have.

Do you believe in the doctrines of Holy Scripture, as set forth in the Articles of Religion of the Methodist Episcopal Church?

Answ. I do.

Will you cheerfully be governed by the rules of the Methodist Episcopal Church, hold sacred the ordinances of God, and endeavor, as much as in you lies, to promote the welfare of your brethren and the advancement of the Redeemer's kingdom?

Answ. I will.

Will you contribute of your earthly substance, according to your ability, to the support of the Gospel and the various benevolent enterprises of the Church?

Answ. I will.

Then the Minister, addressing the Church, shall say:—

Brethren, you have heard the responses given to our inquiries. Have any of you reason to allege why these persons should not be received into full membership in the Church?

No objection being alleged, the Minister shall say to the Candidates:—

We welcome you to the communion of the Church of God; and, in testimony of our Christian affection and the cordiality with which we receive you, I hereby extend to you the right hand of fellowship;

and may God grant that you may be *a* faithful and useful *member* of the Church militant till you are called to the fellowship of the Church triumphant, which is "without fault before the throne of God."

Then shall the Minister offer extemporary Prayer.

The Lord's Supper.

[The General Conference recommends the use of pure, unfermented juice of the grape on Sacramental occasions.]

¶ **484.** ORDER FOR THE ADMINISTRATION OF THE LORD'S SUPPER.

The Elder shall say one or more of these sentences, during the reading of which the persons appointed for that purpose shall receive the alms for the poor:—

LET your light so shine before men, that they may see your good works, and glorify your Father which is in heaven. [Matt. v, 16.]

Lay not up for yourselves treasures upon earth, where moth and rust doth corrupt, and where thieves break through and steal: but lay up for yourselves treasures in heaven, where neither moth nor rust doth corrupt, and where thieves do not break through nor steal. [Matt. vi, 19, 20.]

Whatsoever ye would that men should do to you, do ye even so to them: for this is the law and the prophets. [Matt. vii, 12.]

Not every one that saith unto me, Lord, Lord, shall enter into the kingdom of heaven; but he that doeth the will of my Father which is in heaven. [Matt. vii, 21.]

Zaccheus stood, and said unto the Lord, Behold, Lord, the half of my goods I give to the poor; and if I have taken any thing from any man by false accusation, I restore him fourfold. [Luke xix, 8.]

He which soweth sparingly shall reap also sparingly; and he which soweth bountifully shall reap also bountifully. Every man according as he purposeth in his heart, so let him give; not grudgingly, or of necessity, for God loveth a cheerful giver. [2 Cor. ix, 6, 7.]

As we have therefore opportunity, let us do good unto all men, especially unto them who are of the household of faith. [Gal. vi, 10.]

Godliness with contentment is great gain; for we brought nothing into this world, and it is certain we can carry nothing out. [1 Tim. vi, 6, 7.]

Charge them that are rich in this world, that they be not high-minded, nor trust in uncertain riches, but in the living God, who giveth us richly all things to enjoy; that they do good, that they be rich in good works, ready to distribute, willing to communicate; laying up in store for themselves a good foundation against the time to come, that they may lay hold on eternal life. [1 Tim. vi, 17–19.]

God is not unrighteous to forget your work and labor of love, which ye have showed toward his name, in that ye have ministered to the saints, and do minister. [Heb. vi, 10.]

To do good, and to communicate, forget not; for with such sacrifices God is well pleased. [Heb. xiii, 16.]

Whoso hath this world's good, and seeth his brother have need, and shutteth up his bowels of compassion from him, how dwelleth the love of God in him? [1 John iii, 17.]

He that hath pity upon the poor, lendeth unto the Lord; and that which he hath given will he pay him again. [Prov xix, 17.]

Blessed is he that considereth the poor: the Lord will deliver him in time of trouble. [Psa. xli, 1.]

After which the Elder shall give the following INVITATION, *the people standing:—*

If any man sin, we have an advocate with the Father, Jesus Christ the righteous: and he is the propitiation for our sins: and not for ours only, but also for the sins of the whole world.

Wherefore ye that do truly and earnestly repent of your sins, and are in love and charity with your neighbors, and intend to lead a new life, following the commandments of God, and walking from henceforth in his holy ways; draw near with faith, and take this holy sacrament to your comfort: and, devoutly kneeling, make your humble confession to Almighty God.

Then shall this general CONFESSION *be made by the Minister in the name of all those who are minded to receive the holy communion, both he and all the people devoutly kneeling, and saying:—*

Almighty God, Father of our Lord Jesus Christ, Maker of all things, Judge of all men: we acknowledge and bewail our manifold sins and wickedness, which we from time to time most grievously have committed, by thought, word, and deed, against thy Divine Majesty, provoking most justly thy wrath and indignation against us. We do earnestly repent, and are heartily sorry for these our misdoings; the remembrance of them is grievous unto us. Have mercy upon us, have mercy upon us, most merciful Father; for thy Son, our Lord Jesus Christ's sake, forgive us all that is past, and grant that we may ever hereafter serve and please thee in newness of life, to the honor and glory of thy name, through Jesus Christ our Lord. *Amen.*

Then shall the Elder say,—

Almighty God, our heavenly Father, who of thy great mercy hast promised forgiveness of sins to all them that with hearty repentance and true faith turn unto thee: have mercy upon us; pardon and deliver us from all our sins, confirm and strengthen us in all goodness, and bring us to everlasting life through Jesus Christ our Loid. *Amen.*

The Collect.

Almighty God, unto whom all hearts are open, all desires known, and from whom no secrets are hid; cleanse the thoughts of our hearts by the inspiration of thy Holy Spirit, that we may perfectly love thee, and worthily magnify thy holy name through Jesus Christ our Lord. *Amen.*

Then shall the Elder say,—

We do not presume to come to this thy table, O merciful Lord, trusting in our own righteousness, but in thy manifold and great mercies. We are not worthy so much as to gather up the crumbs under thy table. But thou art the same Lord, whose property is always to have mercy: Grant us, therefore, gracious Lord, so to eat the flesh of thy dear Son Jesus Christ, and to drink his blood, that we may live and grow thereby; and that, being washed through his most precious blood, we may evermore dwell in him, and he in us. *Amen.*

Then the Elder shall say the prayer of CONSECRATION *as followeth:—*

Almighty God, our heavenly Father, who of thy tender mercy didst give thine only Son Jesus Christ to suffer death upon the cross for our redemption; who made there, by his oblation of himself once offered, a full, perfect, and sufficient sacrifice, oblation, and satisfaction for the sins of the whole world; and did institute, and in his holy Gospel command us to continue, a perpetual memory of his precious death until his coming again: hear us, O merciful Father, we most humbly beseech thee, and grant that we, receiving these thy creatures of bread and wine, according to thy Son our Saviour Jesus Christ's holy institution, in remembrance of his death and passion, may be partakers of his most blessed body and blood; who, in the same night that he was betrayed, took bread; (1) and when he had given thanks, he broke it, and gave it to his disciples, saying, Take, eat; this is my body which is given for you; do this in remembrance of me.

(1) *Here the Elder may take the plate of bread in his hand.*

Likewise after supper he took (2) the cup; and when he had given thanks, he gave it to them, saying, Drink ye all of this; for this is my blood of the New Testament, which is shed for you, and for many, for the remission of sins; do this, as oft as ye shall drink it, in remembrance of me. *Amen.*

(2) *Here he may take the cup in his hand.*

Then shall the Minister receive the communion in both kinds, and proceed to deliver the same to the other Ministers, (if any be present;) after which he shall say:—

It is very meet, right, and our bounden duty, that we should at all times, and in all places, give thanks unto thee, O Lord, holy Father, almighty, everlasting God.

Therefore with angels and archangels, and with all the company of heaven, we laud and magnify thy glorious name, evermore praising thee, and saying, Holy, holy, holy Lord God of hosts, heaven and earth are full of thy glory. Glory be to thee, O Lord most high. *Amen.*

The Minister shall then proceed to administer the communion to the people in order, kneeling, into their uncovered hands. And when he delivereth the bread, he shall say:—

The body of our Lord Jesus Christ, which was given for *thee*, preserve *thy soul* and *body* unto everlasting life. Take and eat this in remembrance that Christ died for *thee*, and feed on him in *thy heart* by faith with thanksgiving.

And the Minister that delivereth the cup shall say:

The blood of our Lord Jesus Christ, which was shed for *thee*, preserve *thy soul* and *body* unto everlasting life. Drink this in remembrance that Christ's blood was shed for *thee*, and be thankful.

[If the consecrated bread or wine be all spent before all have communed, the Elder may consecrate more by repeating the Prayer of Consecration.]

[When all have communed, the Minister shall return to the Lord's table, and place upon it what remaineth of the consecrated elements, covering the same with a fair linen cloth.]

Then shall the Elder say the Lord's Prayer; the people kneeling, and repeating after him every petition.

Our Father who art in heaven, hallowed be thy name. Thy kingdom come. Thy will be done in earth, as it is in heaven. Give us this day our daily bread; and forgive us our trespasses, as we forgive them that trespass against us; and lead us not into temptation, but deliver us from evil; for thine is the kingdom, and the power, and the glory, forever. *Amen.*

After which shall be said as followeth:—

O Lord our heavenly Father, we thy humble servants desire thy Fatherly goodness mercifully to accept this our sacrifice of praise and thanksgiving; most humbly beseeching thee to grant, that, by the merits and death of thy Son Jesus Christ, and through faith in his blood, we and thy whole Church may obtain remission of our sins, and all other benefits of his passion. And here we offer and present unto thee, O Lord, ourselves, our souls and bodies, to be a reasonable, holy, and lively sacrifice unto thee; humbly beseeching thee that all we who are partakers of this holy communion may be filled with thy grace and heavenly benediction. And although we be unworthy, through our manifold sins, to offer unto thee any sacrifice, yet we beseech thee to accept this our bounden duty and service; not weighing our merits, but pardoning our offenses, through Jesus Christ our Lord; by whom, and with whom, in the unity of the Holy Ghost, all honor and glory be unto thee, O Father Almighty, world without end. *Amen.*

Then shall be said or sung:—

Glory be to God on high, and on earth peace, good-will toward men. We praise thee, we bless thee, we worship thee, we glorify thee, we give thanks unto thee for thy great glory, O Lord God, heavenly King, God the Father Almighty.

O Lord, the only begotten Son Jesus Christ; O Lord God, Lamb of God, Son of the Father, that takest away the sins of the world, have mercy upon us. Thou that takest away the sins of the world, have mercy upon us. Thou that takest away the sins of the world, receive our prayer. Thou that sittest at the right hand of God the Father, have mercy upon us. For thou only art holy; thou only art the Lord; thou only, O Christ, with the Holy Ghost, art most high in the glory of God the Father. *Amen.*

Then the Elder, if he see it expedient, may put up an extemporary prayer; and afterward shall let the people depart with this blessing:—

May the peace of God, which passeth all understanding, keep your hearts and minds in the knowledge and love of God, and of his Son Jesus Christ our Lord. and the blessing of God Almighty, the

Father, the Son, and the Holy Ghost, be among you, and remain with you always. *Amen.*

N. B. If the Elder be straitened for time, he may omit any part of the service, except the Invitation, the Confession, and the Prayer of Consecration.

Matrimony.

¶ 485. FORM OF THE SOLEMNIZATION OF MATRIMONY.

[The parts in brackets throughout may be used or not at discretion.]

At the day and time appointed for the solemnization of matrimony, the persons to be married—having been qualified according to law—standing together, the man on the right hand and the woman on the left, the Minister shall say:—

DEARLY BELOVED: We are gathered together here in the sight of God, and in the presence of these witnesses, to join together this man and this woman in holy matrimony; which is an honorable estate, instituted of God in the time of man's innocency, signifying unto us the mystical union that is between Christ and his Church; which holy estate Christ adorned and beautified with his presence, and first miracle that he wrought, in Cana of Galilee, and is commended of St. Paul to be honorable among all men; and therefore is not by any to be entered into unadvisedly, but reverently, discreetly, and in the fear of God.

Into which holy estate these two persons present come now to be joined. Therefore if any can show just cause why they may not lawfully be joined together, let him now speak, or else hereafter forever hold his peace.

[*And also speaking unto the persons that are to be married, he shall say:—*

I require and charge you both, that if either of you know any impediment why you may not be lawfully joined together in matrimony, you do now confess it, for be ye well assured, that so many as are coupled together otherwise than God's word doth allow, are not joined together by God, neither is their matrimony lawful.]

If no impediment be alleged, then shall the Minister say unto the man,—

M., wilt thou have this woman to be thy wedded wife, to live together after

God's ordinance in the holy estate of matrimony? Wilt thou love her, comfort her, honor and keep her, in sickness and in health: and forsaking all other, keep thee only unto her, so long as ye both shall live?

The man shall answer,—

I will.

Then shall the Minister say unto the woman,—

N., wilt thou have this man to be thy wedded husband, to live together after God's ordinance, in the holy estate of matrimony? Wilt thou love, honor, and keep him, in sickness and in health: and forsaking all other, keep thee only unto him, so long as ye both shall live?

The woman shall answer,—

I will.

[*Then the Minister shall cause the man with his right hand to take the woman by her right hand, and to say after him as followeth:—*

I, *M.*, take thee, *N.*, to be my wedded wife, to have and to hold, from this day forward, for better, for worse, for richer, for poorer, in sickness and in health, to love and to cherish, till death us do part, according to God's holy ordinance: and thereto I plight thee my faith.

Then shall they loose their hands, and the woman with her right hand taking the man by his right hand, shall likewise say after the Minister:—

I, *N.*, take thee, *M.*, to be my wedded husband, to have and to hold, from this day forward, for better, for worse, for richer, for poorer, in sickness and in health, to love and to cherish, till death us do part, according to God's holy ordinance: and thereto I plight thee my faith.]

Then shall the Minister say:—

O eternal God, Creator and Preserver of all mankind, Giver of all spiritual grace, the Author of everlasting life; send thy blessing upon these thy servants, this man and this woman, whom we bless in thy name; that as Isaac and Rebecca lived faithfully together, so these persons may surely perform and keep the vow and covenant between them made, and may ever remain in perfect love and peace together, and live according to thy laws, through Jesus Christ our Lord. *Amen.*

[*If the parties desire it, the man shall here hand a ring to the Minister, who shall return it to him, and direct him to place it on the third finger of the woman's left hand. And the man shall say to the woman, repeating after the Minister,—*

With this ring I thee wed, and with my worldly goods I thee endow, in the name of the Father, and of the Son, and of the Holy Ghost. *Amen.*]

Then shall the Minister join their right hands together, and say:—

Forasmuch as *M.* and *N.* have consented together in holy wedlock, and have witnessed the same before God and this company, and thereto have pledged their faith either to other, and have declared the same by joining of hands; I pronounce that they are husband and wife together, in the name of the Father, and of the Son, and of the Holy Ghost. Those whom God hath joined together, let no man put asunder. *Amen.*

And the Minister shall add this blessing:—

God, the Father, the Son, and the Holy Ghost, bless, preserve, and keep you; the Lord mercifully with his favor look upon you, and so fill you with all spiritual benediction and grace, that ye may so live together in this life, that in the world to come ye may have life everlasting. *Amen.*

Then shall the Minister offer the following prayer.

O God of Abraham, God of Isaac, God of Jacob, bless this man and this woman, and sow the seed of eternal life in their hearts, that whatsoever in thy holy word they shall profitably learn, they may indeed fulfill the same. Look, O Lord, mercifully on them from heaven, and bless them: as thou didst send thy blessings upon Abraham and Sarah to their great comfort, so vouchsafe to send thy blessings upon this man and this woman, that they, obeying thy will, and always being in safety under thy protection, may abide in thy love unto their lives' end, through Jesus Christ our Lord.

Almighty God, who at the beginning didst create our first parents, Adam and Eve, and didst sanctify and join them together in marriage, pour upon these persons the riches of thy grace, sanctify and bless them, that they may please thee both in body and soul, and live together in holy love unto their lives' end. *Amen.*

Here the Minister may use extemporary prayer.

Then the Minister shall say,—

Our Father who art in heaven, hallowed be thy name. Thy kingdom come. Thy will be done in earth as it is in heaven. Give us this day our daily bread; and forgive us our trespasses, as we forgive them that trespass against us; and lead us not into temptation, but deliver us from evil; for thine is the kingdom, and the power, and the glory, forever. *Amen.*

Burial of the Dead.

¶ 486. FORM FOR THE BURIAL OF THE DEAD.

The Minister, going before the corpse, shall say,—

I AM the resurrection, and the life: he that believeth in me, though he were dead, yet shall he live; and whosoever liveth and believeth in me shall never die. [John xi, 25, 26.]

I know that my Redeemer liveth, and that he shall stand at the latter day upon the earth: and though after my skin worms destroy this body, yet in my flesh shall I see God: whom I shall see for myself, and mine eyes shall behold, and not another. [Job xix, 25–27.]

We brought nothing into this world, and it is certain we can carry nothing out. The Lord gave, and the Lord hath taken away; blessed be the name of the Lord. [1 Tim. vi, 7; Job i, 21.]

In the house or church may be read one or both of the following Psalms, or some other suitable portion of Scripture.

Psalm xxxix:

I said, I will take heed to my ways, that I sin not with my tongue: I will keep my mouth with a bridle, while the wicked is before me. I was dumb with silence, I held my peace, even from good; and my sorrow was stirred. My heart was hot within me; while I was musing the fire burned: then spake I with my tongue, Lord, make me to know mine end, and the measure of my days, what it is; that I may know how frail I am. Behold, thou hast made my days as a handbreadth; and mine age is as nothing before thee: verily every man at his best state is altogether vanity. Surely every man walketh in a vain show: surely they are disquieted in vain: he heapeth up riches, and knoweth not who shall gather them. And now, Lord, what wait I for? my hope is in thee. Deliver me from all my transgressions: make me not the reproach of the foolish. I was dumb, I opened not my mouth; because thou didst it. Remove thy stroke away from me: I am consumed by the blow of thine hand. When thou with rebukes dost correct man for iniquity, thou makest his beauty to consume away like a moth: surely every man is vanity. Hear my prayer, O Lord, and give ear unto my cry; hold not thy peace at my tears: for I am a stranger with thee, and a sojourner, as all my fathers were. O spare me, that I may recover strength, before I go hence, and be no more.

Psalm xc:

Lord, thou hast been our dwelling-place in all generations. Before the mountains were brought forth, or ever thou hadst formed the earth and the world, even from everlasting to everlasting, thou art God. Thou turnest man to destruction; and sayest, Return, ye children of men. For a thousand years in thy sight are but as yesterday when it is past, and as a watch in the night. Thou carriest them away as with a flood; they are as a sleep: in the morning they are like grass which groweth up. In the morning it flourisheth, and groweth up; in the evening it is cut down, and withereth. For we are consumed by thine anger, and by thy wrath are we troubled. Thou hast set our iniquities before thee, our secret sins in the light of thy countenance. For all our days are passed away in thy wrath: we spend our years as a tale that is told. The days of our years are threescore years and ten; and if by reason of strength they be fourscore years, yet is their strength labor and sorrow; for it is soon cut off, and we fly away. Who knoweth the power of thine anger? even according to thy fear, so is thy wrath. So teach us to number our days, that we may apply our hearts unto wisdom. Return, O Lord, how long? and let it repent thee concerning thy servants. O satisfy us early with thy mercy; that we may rejoice and be glad all our days. Make us glad according to the days wherein thou hast afflicted us, and the years wherein we have seen evil. Let thy work appear unto thy servants, and thy glory unto their children. And let the beauty of the Lord our God be upon us: and establish thou the work of our hands upon us; yea, the works of our hands establish thou it.

Then may follow the reading of the Epistle as follows:—

1 Cor. xv, 41–58:

There is one glory of the sun, and another glory of the moon, and another glory of the stars; for one star differeth from another star in glory. So also is the resurrection of the dead. It is sown in corruption, it is raised in incorruption: it is sown in dishonor, it is raised in glory: it is sown in weakness, it is raised in power: it is sown a natural body, it is raised a spiritual body. There is a natural body, and there is a spiritual body. And so it is written, The first man Adam was made a living soul; the last Adam was made a quickening spirit. Howbeit that was not first which is spiritual, but that which is natural; and afterward that which is spiritual. The first man is of the earth, earthy: the second man is the Lord from heaven. As is the earthy, such are they also that are earthy: and as is the heavenly, such are they also that are heavenly. And as we have borne the image of the earthy, we shall also bear the image of the heavenly. Now this I say, brethren, that flesh and blood cannot inherit the kingdom of God; neither doth corruption inherit incorruption. Behold, I show you a mystery; We shall not all sleep, but we shall all be changed, in a moment, in the twinkling of an eye, at the last trump: for the trumpet shall sound, and the dead shall be raised incorruptible, and we shall be changed. For this corruptible must put on incorruption, and this mortal must put on immortality. So when this corruptible shall have put on incorruption, and this mortal shall have put on immortality, then shall be brought to pass the saying that is written, Death is swallowed up in victory. O death, where is thy sting? O grave, where is thy victory? The sting of death is sin; and the strength of sin is the law. But thanks be to God, which giveth us the victory through our Lord Jesus Christ. Therefore, my beloved brethren, be ye steadfast, unmovable, always abounding in the work of the Lord, forasmuch as ye know that your labor is not in vain in the Lord.

At the grave, when the corpse is laid in the earth, the Minister shall say,—

Man that is born of a woman hath but a short time to live, and is full of misery. He cometh up, and is cut down like a flower: he fleeth as it were a shadow, and never continueth in one stay.

In the midst of life we are in death: of whom may we seek for succor, but of thee, O Lord, who for our sins art justly displeased?

Yet, O Lord God most holy, O Lord most mighty, O holy and most merciful Saviour, deliver us not into the bitter pains of eternal death.

Thou knowest, Lord, the secrets of our hearts; shut not thy merciful ears to our prayers, but spare us, Lord most holy, O God most mighty, O holy and merciful Saviour, thou most worthy Judge eternal, suffer us not at our last hour for any pains of death to fall from thee.

Then, while the earth shall be cast upon the body by some standing by, the Minister shall say,—

Forasmuch as it hath pleased Almighty God, in his wise providence, to take out of the world the soul of the departed, we therefore commit *his* body to the ground; earth to earth, ashes to ashes, dust to dust; looking for the general resurrection in the last day, and the life of the world to come, through our Lord Jesus Christ; at whose second coming in glorious majesty to judge the world, the earth and the sea shall give up their dead; and the corruptible bodies of those who sleep in him shall be changed and made like unto his own glorious body; according to the mighty working whereby he is able to subdue all things unto himself.

Then shall be said:—

I heard a voice from heaven saying unto me, Write, From henceforth blessed are the dead who die in the Lord: Even so, saith the Spirit; for they rest from their labors.

Then shall the Minister say,

Lord, have mercy upon us.
Christ, have mercy upon us.
Lord, have mercy upon us.

The Collect.

O merciful God, the Father of our Lord Jesus Christ, who is the resurrection and the life: in whom whosoever believeth shall live, though he die, and whosoever liveth and believeth in Him shall not die eternally; We meekly beseech thee, O Father, to raise us from the death of sin unto the life of righteousness; that when we shall depart this life we may rest in him; and at the general resurrection on the last day may be found acceptable in thy sight, and receive that blessing which thy well-beloved Son shall then pronounce to all that love and fear thee, saying, Come, ye blessed children of my Father, receive the kingdom prepared for you from the beginning of the world. Grant this, we beseech thee, O merciful Father, through Jesus Christ our Mediator and Redeemer. *Amen.*

Our Father who art in heaven, hallowed be thy name. Thy kingdom come. Thy will be done in earth, as it is in heaven. Give us this day our daily bread; and forgive us our trespasses as we forgive them that trespass against us;

and lead us not into temptation, but deliver us from evil: for thine is the kingdom, and the power, and the glory, for ever. *Amen.*

The grace of our Lord Jesus Christ, and the love of God, and the fellowship of the Holy Ghost, be with us all evermore. *Amen.*

Ordination.

¶ 487. THE FORM OF CONSECRATING BISHOPS.

The Collect.

ALMIGHTY GOD, who by thy Son Jesus Christ didst give to thy holy apostles, elders, and evangelists, many excellent gifts, and didst charge them to feed thy flock; give grace, we beseech thee, to all the ministers and pastors of thy Church, that they may diligently preach thy word and duly administer the godly discipline thereof; and grant to the people that they may obediently follow the same, that all may receive the crown of everlasting glory, through Jesus Christ our Lord. *Amen.*

Then shall be read by one of the Elders—

The Epistle. Acts xx, 17-35.

From Miletus Paul sent to Ephesus, and called the elders of the Church

And when they were come to him, he said unto them, Ye know, from the first day that I came into Asia, after what manner I have been with you at all seasons, serving the Lord with all humility of mind, and with many tears, and temptations, which befell me by the lying in wait of the Jews: and how I kept back nothing that was profitable unto you, but have showed you, and have taught you publicly, and from house to house, testifying both to the Jews, and also to the Greeks, repentance toward God, and faith toward our Lord Jesus Christ. And now, behold, I go bound in the spirit unto Jerusalem, not knowing the things that shall befall me there: save that the Holy Ghost witnesseth in every city, saying that bonds and afflictions abide me. But none of these things move me, neither count I my life dear unto myself, so that I might finish my course with joy, and the ministry, which I have received of the Lord Jesus, to testify the Gospel of the grace of God. And now, behold, I know that ye all, among whom I have gone preaching the kingdom of God, shall see my face no more. Wherefore I take you to record this day, that I am pure from the blood of all men. For I have not shunned to declare unto you all the counsel of God. Take heed therefore unto yourselves, and to all the flock, over the which the Holy Ghost hath made you overseers, to feed the Church of God which he hath purchased with his own blood. For I know this, that after my departing shall grievous wolves enter in among you, not sparing the flock. Also of your own selves shall men arise, speaking perverse things, to draw away disciples after them. Therefore watch, and remember, that by the space of three years I ceased not to warn every one night and day with tears. And now, brethren, I commend you to God, and to the word of his grace, which is able to build you up, and to give you an inheritance among all them which are sanctified. I have coveted no man's silver, or gold, or apparel. Yea, ye yourselves know, that these hands have ministered unto my necessities, and to them that were with me. I have showed you all things, how that so laboring ye ought to support the weak, and to remember the words of the Lord Jesus, how he said, It is more blessed to give than to receive.

Then another shall read—

The Gospel. St. John xxi, 15–17.

Jesus saith to Simon Peter, Simon, son of Jonas, lovest thou me more than these? He saith unto him, Yea, Lord; thou knowest that I love thee. He saith unto him, Feed my lambs. He saith to him again the second time, Simon, son of Jonas, lovest thou me? He saith unto him, Yea, Lord; thou knowest that I love thee. He saith unto him, Feed my sheep. He saith unto him the third time, Simon, son of Jonas, lovest thou me? Peter was grieved because he said unto him the third time, Lovest thou me? And he said unto him, Lord, thou knowest all things; thou knowest that I love thee. Jesus saith unto him, Feed my sheep.

Or this: St. Matt. xxviii, 18–20.

Jesus came and spake unto them, saying, All power is given unto me in heaven and in earth. Go ye therefore, and teach all nations, baptizing them in the name of the Father, and of the Son, and of the Holy Ghost: teaching them to observe all things whatsoever I have commanded you: and, lo, I am with you alway, even unto the end of the world.

After the Gospel and the Sermon are ended, the elected person shall be presented by two Elders unto the Bishop, saying,—

We present unto you this holy man to be consecrated a Bishop.

Then the Bishop shall move the congregation present to pray, saying thus to them :—

Brethren, it is written in the Gospel of St. Luke, that our Saviour Christ continued the whole night in prayer before he did choose and send forth his twelve apostles. It is written also in the Acts of the Apostles, that the disciples who were at Antioch did fast and pray before they laid hands on Paul and Barnabas, and sent them forth on their first mission to the Gentiles. Let us, therefore, following the example of our Saviour Christ, and his apostles, first fall to prayer before we admit, and send forth this person presented to us, to the work whereunto we trust the Holy Ghost hath called him.

Then shall be said this prayer following :—

Almighty God, giver of all good things, who by thy Holy Spirit hast appointed divers offices in thy Church: mercifully behold this thy servant now called to the work and ministry of a Bishop, and replenish him so with the truth of thy doctrine, and adorn him with innocency of life, that both by word and deed he may faithfully serve thee in this office, to the glory of thy name, and the edifying and well governing of thy Church, through the merits of our Saviour Jesus Christ, who liveth and reigneth with thee, and the Holy Ghost, world without end. *Amen.*

Then the Bishop shall say to him that is to be consecrated:—

Brother, forasmuch as the Holy Scripture commands that we should not be hasty in laying on hands, and admitting any person to government in the Church of Christ, which he hath purchased with no less price than the shedding of his own blood; before you are admitted to this administration, you will, in the fear of God, give answer to the questions which I now propound:—

Are you persuaded that you are truly called to this ministration, according to the will of our Lord Jesus Christ?

Answ. I am so persuaded.

The Bishop. Are you persuaded that the Holy Scriptures contain sufficiently all doctrine required of necessity for eternal salvation, through faith in Jesus Christ? And are you determined, out of the same Holy Scriptures, to instruct the people committed to your charge, and to teach or maintain nothing as required of necessity to eternal salvation but that which you shall be persuaded may be concluded and proved by the same?

Answ. I am so persuaded and determined, by God's grace.

The Bishop. Will you then faithfully exercise yourself in the same Holy Scriptures, and call upon God by prayer for the true understanding of the same, so that you may be able by them to teach and exhort with wholesome doctrine, and to withstand and convince the gainsayers?

Answ. I will do so, by the help of God.

The Bishop. Are you ready with faithful diligence to banish and drive away all erroneous and strange doctrines contrary to God's word, and both privately and openly to call upon and encourage others to the same?

Answ. I am ready, the Lord being my helper.

The Bishop. Will you deny all ungodliness and worldly lust, and live soberly, righteously, and godly, in this present world, that you may show yourself in all things an example of good works unto others, that the adversary may be ashamed, having nothing to say against you?

Answ. I will so do, the Lord being my helper.

The Bishop. Will you maintain and set forward, as much as shall lie in you, quietness, love, and peace among all men: and such as shall be unquiet, disobedient, and criminal, correct and punish according to such authority as you have by God's word, and as shall be committed unto you?

Answ. I will so do, by the help of God.

The Bishop. Will you be faithful in ordaining, or laying hands upon and sending others, and in all the other duties of your office?

Answ. I will so be, by the help of God.

The Bishop. Will you show yourself

gentle, and be merciful for Christ's sake, to poor and needy people, and to all strangers destitute of help?

Answ. I will so show myself, by God's help.

Then the Bishop shall say,—

Almighty God, our heavenly Father, who hath given you a good will to do all these things, grant also unto you strength and power to perform the same, that he accomplishing in you the good work which he hath begun, you may be found blameless at the last day, through Jesus Christ our Lord. *Amen.*

Then shall Veni, Creator Spiritus, be said.

Come, Holy Ghost, our souls inspire,
And lighten with celestial fire.
Thou the anointing Spirit art,
Who dost thy sevenfold gifts impart.
Thy blessed unction from above
Is comfort, life, and fire of love.
Enable with perpetual light
The dullness of our blinded sight;
Anoint and cheer our soiléd face
With the abundance of thy grace;
Keep far our foes, give peace at home;
Where thou art Guide, no ill can come.

Teach us to know the Father, Son,
And thee of both to be but one;
That through the ages all along,
This may be our endless song:
Praise to thy eternal merit,
Father, Son, and Holy Spirit.

That ended, the Bishop shall say,—

Lord, hear our prayer.
Answ. And let our cry come unto thee

Bishop.

Let us pray.

Almighty God and most merciful Father, who of thine infinite goodness hast given thine only and dearly beloved Son Jesus Christ to be our Redeemer, and the author of everlasting life; who after that he had made perfect our redemption by his death, and was ascended into heaven, poured down his gifts abundantly upon men, making some apostles, some prophets, some evangelists, some pastors and teachers, to the edifying and making perfect of his Church: grant, we beseech thee, to this thy servant, such grace that he may evermore be ready to spread abroad thy Gospel, the glad tidings of reconciliation with thee, and use the authority given him, not to destruction, but to salvation; not to hurt, but to help; so that as a wise and faithful servant, giving to the family their portion in due season, he may at last be received into everlasting joy, through Jesus Christ our Lord, who, with thee and the Holy Ghost, liveth and reigneth, one God world without end. *Amen.*

Then the Bishop and Elders present shall lay their hands upon the head of the elected person, kneeling before them, the Bishop saying:—

The Lord pour upon thee the Holy Ghost for the office and work of a Bishop in the Church of God now committed unto thee by the authority of the Church through the imposition of our hands, in the name of the Father, and of the Son, and of the Holy Ghost. *Amen.* And remember that thou stir up the grace of God which is in thee; for God hath not given us the spirit of fear, but of power, and love, and of a sound mind.

Then the Bishop shall deliver him the Bible, saying:—

Give heed unto reading, exhortation, and doctrine. Think upon the things contained in this book. Be diligent in them, that the increase coming thereby may be manifest unto all men. Take heed unto thyself, and to thy doctrine; for by so doing thou shalt both save thyself and them that hear thee. Be to the flock of Christ a shepherd, not a wolf; feed them, devour them not. Hold up the weak, heal the sick, bind up the broken, bring again the outcast, seek the lost, be so merciful that you may not be too remiss; so minister discipline that you forget not mercy; that when the chief Shepherd shall appear, you may receive the never-fading crown of glory, through Jesus Christ our Lord. *Amen.*

[Then the Bishop shall administer the Lord's Supper to the newly-consecrated Bishop and other persons present.]

Then shall be said the following prayers:—

Most merciful Father, we beseech thee to send down upon this thy servant thy heavenly blessing, and so endue him with thy holy Spirit, that he, preaching thy word, and exercising authority in thy Church, may not only be earnest to reprove, beseech, and rebuke with all patience and doctrine, but also may be to such as believe a wholesome example in word, in conversation, in love, in faith, and in purity: that faithfully fulfilling his course, at the last day he may receive the crown of righteousness laid up by the Lord, the righteous Judge, who liveth and reigneth, one God with the Father and the Holy Ghost, world without end. *Amen.*

Prevent us, O Lord, in all our doings with thy most gracious favor, and further us with thy continual help, that in all our works begun, continued, and ended in thee, we may glorify thy holy name; and finally, by thy mercy, obtain everlasting life through Jesus Christ our Lord. *Amen.*

The peace of God, which passeth all understanding, keep your hearts and minds in the knowledge and love of God, and of his Son Jesus Christ our Lord; and the blessing of God Almighty, the Father, the Son, and the Holy Ghost, be among you, and remain with you always. *Amen.*

¶ 488. THE FORM OF ORDAINING ELDERS.

[When the day appointed by the Bishop is come, there shall be a sermon or exhortation, declaring the duty and office of such as come to be admitted Elders; how necessary that order is in the Church of Christ, and also how the people ought to esteem them in their office.]

After which, one of the Elders shall present unto the Bishop all them that are to be ordained, and say,—

I present unto you these persons to be ordained Elders.

Then their names being read aloud, the Bishop shall say unto the people,—

Brethren, these are they whom we purpose, God willing, this day to ordain Elders. For after due examination, we find not to the contrary, but that they are lawfully called to this function and ministry, and that they are persons meet for the same. But if there be any of you who knoweth any crime or impediment in any of them, for the which he ought not to be received into this holy ministry, let him come forth in the name of God, and show what the crime or impediment is.

[If any crime or impediment be objected, the Bishop shall surcease from ordaining that person until such time as the party accused shall be found clear of the same.]

Then shall be said the Collect, Epistle, and Gospel, as followeth :—

The Collect.

Almighty God, giver of all good things, who by thy Holy Spirit hast appointed divers orders of ministers in thy Church; mercifully behold these thy servants now called to the office of Elders, and replenish them so with the truth of thy doctrine, and adorn them with innocency of life, that both by word and good example they may faithfully serve thee in this office, to the glory of thy name, and the edification of thy Church, through the merits of our Saviour Jesus Christ who liveth and reigneth with thee and the Holy Ghost, world without end. *Amen.*

The Epistle. Eph. iv, 7–13.

Unto every one of us is given grace according to the measure of the gift of Christ. Wherefore he saith, When he ascended up on high, he led captivity captive, and gave gifts unto men. Now that he ascended, what is it but that he also descended first into the lower parts of the earth? He that descended is the same also that ascended up far above all heavens, that he might fill all things. And he gave some, apostles; and some, prophets; and some, evangelists; and some, pastors and teachers; for the perfecting of the saints, for the work of the ministry, for the edifying of the body of Christ: till we all come in the unity of the faith, and of the knowledge of the Son of God, unto a perfect man, unto the measure of the stature of the fullness of Christ

After this shall be read for the Gospel, part of the tenth chapter of St. John.

St. John x, 1–16.

Verily, verily, I say unto you, He that entereth not by the door into the sheepfold, but climbeth up some other way, the same is a thief and a robber. But he that entereth in by the door is the shepherd of the sheep. To him the porter openeth; and the sheep hear his voice: and he calleth his own sheep by name, and leadeth them out. And when he putteth forth his own sheep, he goeth before them, and the sheep follow him; for they know his voice. And a stranger will they not follow, but will flee from him; for they know not the voice of strangers. This parable spake Jesus unto them; but they understood not what things they were which he spake unto them. Then said Jesus unto them again, Verily, verily, I say unto you, I am the door of the sheep. All that ever came before me are thieves and robbers: but the sheep did not hear them. I am the door: by me if any man enter in, he shall be saved, and shall go in and out, and find pasture. The thief cometh not but for to steal, and to kill, and to destroy: I am come that they might have life, and that they might have it more abundantly. I am the good shepherd: the good shepherd giveth his life for the sheep. But he that is a hireling, and not the shepherd, whose own the sheep are not, seeth the wolf coming, and leaveth the sheep, and fleeth; and the wolf catcheth them, and scattereth the sheep. The hireling fleeth, because he is a hireling, and careth not for the sheep. I am the good shepherd, and know my sheep, and am known of mine. As the Father knoweth me, even so know I the Father: and I lay down my life for the sheep. And other sheep I have, which are not of this fold. them also I must bring, and they shall hear my voice; and there shall be one fold and one shepherd.

And that done, the Bishop shall say unto them as hereafter followeth :—

You have heard, brethren, in your private examination, and in the holy lessons taken out of the Gospel and the writings of the apostles, of what dignity and of how great importance this office is whereunto ye are called. And now again we exhort you, in the name of our Lord Jesus Christ, that ye have in remembrance into how high a dignity and to how weighty an office ye are called: that is to say, to be messengers, watchmen, and stewards, of the Lord; to teach and to premonish, to feed, and provide for, the Lord's family; to gather the outcasts, to seek the lost, and to be ever ready to spread abroad the Gospel, the glad tidings of reconciliation with God.

Have always therefore printed in your

remembrance how great a treasure is committed to your charge. For they are the sheep of Christ, which he bought with his death, and for whom he shed his blood. The Church whom you must serve is his spouse and his body. And if it shall happen, the same Church, or any member thereof, do take any hurt or hinderance by reason of your negligence, ye know the greatness of the fault, and also the horrible punishment that will ensue. Wherefore consider with yourselves the end of the ministry toward the children of God, toward the spouse and body of Christ; and see that you never cease your labor, your care and diligence, until you have done all that lieth in you, according to your bounden duty, to bring all such as are or shall be committed to your charge, unto that agreement in the faith and knowledge of God, and to that ripeness and perfectness of age in Christ, that there be no place left among you, either for error in religion, or for viciousness in life.

Forasmuch then as your office is both of so great excellency, and of so great difficulty, ye see with how great care and study ye ought to apply yourselves, as well that ye may show yourselves dutiful and thankful unto that Lord who hath placed you in so high a dignity; as also to beware that neither you yourselves offend, nor be occasion that others offend. Howbeit ye cannot have a mind and will thereto of yourselves, for that will and ability are given of God alone; therefore ye ought, and have need, to pray earnestly for his Holy Spirit. And seeing that ye cannot by any other means compass the doing of so weighty a work, pertaining to the salvation of man, but with doctrine and exhortation taken out of the Holy Scriptures, and with a life agreeable to the same; consider how studious ye ought to be in reading and learning the Scriptures, and in framing the manners, both of yourselves and of them that specially pertain unto you, according to the rule of the same Scriptures; and for this self-same cause, how ye ought to forsake and set aside (as much as you may) all worldly cares and studies.

We have good hope that you have all weighed and pondered these things with yourselves long before this time: and that you have clearly determined, by God's grace, to give yourselves wholly to this office, whereunto it hath pleased God to call you: so that, as much as lieth in you, you will apply yourselves wholly to this one thing, and draw all your cares and studies this way, and that you will continually pray to God the Father, by the mediation of our only Saviour Jesus Christ, for the heavenly assistance of the Holy Ghost; that by daily reading and weighing of the Scriptures, ye may wax riper and stronger in your ministry; and that ye may so endeavor to sanctify the lives of you and yours, and to fashion them after the rule and doctrine of Christ, that ye may be wholesome and godly examples and patterns for the people to follow.

And now that this present congregation of Christ, here assembled, may also understand your minds and wills in these things, and that this your promise may the more move you to do your duties: ye shall answer plainly to these things which we, in the name of God and his Church, shall demand of you touching the same.

Do you think in your heart that you are truly called, according to the will of our Lord Jesus Christ, to the order of Elders?

Answ. I think so.

The Bishop. Are you persuaded that the Holy Scriptures contain sufficiently all doctrine required of necessity for eternal salvation through faith in Jesus Christ? And are you determined out of the said Scriptures to instruct the people committed to your charge, and to teach nothing as required of necessity to eternal salvation, but that which you shall be persuaded may be concluded and proved by the Scriptures?

Answ. I am so persuaded, and have so determined, by God's grace.

The Bishop. Will you then give your faithful diligence always so to minister the doctrine and sacraments, and discipline of Christ, as the Lord hath commanded?

Answ. I will so do, by the help of the Lord.

The Bishop. Will you be ready with all faithful diligence to banish and drive away all erroneous and strange doctrines contrary to God's word; and to use both public and private monitions and exhortations, as well to the sick as to the whole within your charge, as need shall require and occasion shall be given?

Answ. I will, the Lord being my helper.

The Bishop. Will you be diligent in prayers, and in reading of the Holy Scriptures, and in such studies as help to the knowledge of the same, laying aside the study of the world and the flesh?

Answ. I will endeavor so to do, the Lord being my helper.

The Bishop. Will you be diligent to frame and fashion yourselves, and your families, according to the doctrine of Christ: and to make both yourselves and them, as much as in you lieth, wholesome examples and patterns to the flock of Christ?

Answ. I will apply myself thereto, the Lord being my helper.

The Bishop. Will you maintain and set forward, as much as lieth in you, quietness, peace, and love, among all Christian people, and especially among them that are or shall be committed to your charge?

Answ. I will so do, the Lord being my helper.

The Bishop. Will you reverently obey your chief ministers, unto whom is committed the charge and government over you; following with a glad mind and will their godly admonitions, submitting yourselves to their godly judgments?

Answ. I will so do, the Lord being my helper.

Then shall the Bishop, standing up, say,—

Almighty God, who hath given you this will to do all these things, grant also unto you strength and power to perform the same; that he may accomplish his work which he hath begun in you, through Jesus Christ our Lord. *Amen.*

[After this the congregation shall be desired secretly in their prayers to make their humble supplications to God for all these things: for the which prayers there shall be silence kept for a space.]

After which shall be said by the Bishop, (the persons to be ordained Elders all kneeling,) Veni, Creator Spiritus, *the Bishop beginning, and the Elders and others that are present answering by verse, as followeth:—*

Come, Holy Ghost, our souls inspire,
And lighten with celestial fire.
Thou the anointing Spirit art,
Who dost thy sevenfold gifts impart.

Thy blessed unction from above
Is comfort, life, and fire of love.
Enable with perpetual light
The dullness of our blinded sight.
Anoint and cheer our soilèd face
With the abundance of thy grace.
Keep far our foes, give peace at home;
Where thou art Guide no ill can come.
Teach us to know the Father, Son,
And thee of both to be but one;
That through the ages all along,
This may be our endless song:
Praise to thy eternal merit,
Father, Son, and Holy Spirit.

That done, the Bishop shall pray in this wise and say,—

Let us pray.

Almighty God and heavenly Father, who of thine infinite love and goodness toward us, hast given to us thy only and most dearly beloved Son Jesus Christ to be our Redeemer, and the author of everlasting life; who, after he had made perfect our redemption by his death, and was ascended into heaven, sent abroad into the world his apostles, prophets, evangelists, teachers, and pastors, by whose labor and ministry he gathered together a great flock in all parts of the world, to set forth the eternal praise of thy holy name: for these so great benefits of thy eternal goodness, and for that thou hast vouchsafed to call these thy servants here present to the same office and ministry appointed for the salvation of mankind, we render unto thee most hearty thanks: we praise and worship thee; and we humbly beseech thee by the same, thy blessed Son, to grant unto all who either here or elsewhere call upon thy name, that we may continue to show ourselves thankful unto thee for these, and all other thy benefits, and that we may daily increase and go forward in the knowledge and faith of thee and thy Son, by the Holy Spirit. So that as well by these thy ministers, as by them over whom they shall be appointed thy ministers, thy holy name may be forever glorified, and thy blessed kingdom enlarged, through the same, thy Son Jesus Christ our Lord: who liveth and reigneth with thee in the unity of the same Holy Spirit, world without end. *Amen.*

When this prayer is done, the Bishop, with the Elders present, shall lay their hands severally upon the head of every one that receiveth the order of Elders; the receivers humbly kneeling upon their knees, and the Bishop saying,—

The Lord pour upon thee the Holy Ghost for the office and work of an Elder in the Church of God, now committed unto thee by the authority of the Church through the imposition of our hands. And be thou a faithful dispenser of the word of God, and of his holy sacraments; in the name of the Father, and of the Son, and of the Holy Ghost. *Amen.*

Then the Bishop shall deliver to every one of them, kneeling, the Bible into his hands, saying,—

Take thou authority as an Elder in the Church, to preach the word of God, and to administer the holy sacraments in the congregation.

Then the Bishop shall say,—

Most merciful Father, we beseech thee to send upon these thy servants thy heavenly blessings, that they may be clothed with righteousness, and that thy word spoken by their mouths may have such success, that it may never be spoken in vain. Grant also that we may have grace to hear and receive what they shall deliver out of thy most holy word, or agreeably to the same, as the means of our salvation; and that in all our words and deeds we may seek thy glory, and the increase of thy kingdom, through Jesus Christ our Lord. *Amen.*

Prevent us, O Lord, in all our doings, with thy most gracious favor, and further us with thy continual help; that in all our works, begun, continued, and ended in thee, we may glorify thy holy name, and finally, by thy mercy, obtain everlasting life, through Jesus Christ our Lord. *Amen.*

The peace of God, which passeth all understanding, keep your hearts and minds in the knowledge and love of God, and of his Son Jesus Christ our Lord. And the blessing of God Almighty, the Father, the Son, and the Holy Ghost, be among you, and remain with you always. *Amen.*

*** [If on the same day the order of Deacons be given to some, and that of Elders to others, the Deacons shall be first presented, and then the Elders. The Collects shall both be used:

first that for Deacons, then that for Elders. The Epistle shall be Ephes. iv, 7-13, as before in this office: immediately after which, they that are to be ordained Deacons shall be examined and ordained as is above prescribed. Then one of them having read the Gospel, which shall be St. John x, 1-16, as before in this Office, they that are to be ordained Elders shall likewise be examined and ordained, as in this Office before appointed.]

¶ 489. THE FORM OF ORDAINING DEACONS.

[When the day appointed by the Bishop is come, there shall be a sermon or exhortation, declaring the duty and office of such as come to be admitted as Deacons.]

After which, one of the Elders shall present unto the Bishop the persons to be ordained Deacons, and their names being read aloud, the Bishop shall say unto the people :—

BRETHREN, if there be any of you who knoweth any crime or impediment in any of these persons presented to be ordained Deacons, for the which he ought not to be admitted to that office, let him come forth in the name of God, and show what the crime or impediment is.

[If any crime or impediment be objected, the Bishop shall surcease from ordaining that person, until such time as the party accused shall be found clear of the same.]

Then shall be read the following Collect and Epistle :—

The Collect.

Almighty God, who by thy divine Providence hast appointed divers orders of ministers in thy Church, and didst inspire thy apostles to choose into the order of deacons thy first martyr, St. Stephen, with others: mercifully behold these thy servants, now called to the like office and administration; replenish them so with the truth of thy doctrine, and adorn them with innocency of life, that both by word and good example they may faithfully serve thee in this office to the glory of thy name, and the edification of thy Church, through the merits of our Saviour Jesus Christ, who liveth and reigneth with thee and the Holy Ghost, now and forever. *Amen.*

The Epistle. 1 Tim. iii, 8–13.

Likewise must the deacons be grave, not double-tongued, not given to much wine, not greedy of filthy lucre; holding the mystery of the faith in a pure conscience. And let these also first be proved, then let them use the office of a deacon, being found blameless. Even so must their wives be grave, not slanderers, sober, faithful in all things. Let the deacons be the husbands of one wife, ruling their children and their own houses well. For they that have used the office of a deacon well purchase to themselves a good degree, and great boldness in the faith which is in Christ Jesus.

Then shall the Bishop examine every one of those who are to be ordained, in the presence of the people, after this manner following:—

Do you trust that you are inwardly moved by the Holy Ghost to take upon you the office of the ministry in the Church of Christ, to serve God for the promoting of his glory and the edifying of his people?

Answ. I trust so.

The Bishop. Do you unfeignedly believe all the canonical Scriptures of the Old and New Testament?

Answ. I do believe them.

The Bishop. Will you diligently read or expound the same unto the people whom you shall be appointed to serve?

Answ. I will.

The Bishop. It appertaineth to the office of a Deacon to assist the Elder in divine service. And especially when he ministereth the Holy Communion, to help him in the distribution thereof, and to read and expound the Holy Scriptures; to instruct the youth, and to baptize. And furthermore, it is his office to search for the sick, poor, and impotent, that they may be visited and relieved. Will you do this gladly and willingly?

Answ. I will do so, by the help of God.

The Bishop. Will you apply all your diligence to frame and fashion your own lives (and the lives of your families) according to the doctrine of Christ; and to make (both) yourselves, (and them,) as much as in you lieth, wholesome examples of the flock of Christ?

Answ. I will do so, the Lord being my helper.

The Bishop. Will you reverently obey them to whom the charge and government over you is committed, following with a glad mind and will their godly admonitions?

Answ. I will endeavor so to do, the Lord being my helper.

Then the Bishop, laying his hands severally upon the head of every one of them, shall say,—

Take thou authority to execute the office of a Deacon in the Church of God; in the name of the Father, and of the Son, and of the Holy Ghost. *Amen.*

Then shall the Bishop deliver to every one of them the Holy Bible, saying,—

Take thou authority to read the Holy Scriptures in the Church of God, and to preach the same.

Then one appointed by the Bishop shall read the Gospel.

Luke xii, 35–38.

Let your loins be girded about, and your lights burning; and ye yourselves like unto men that wait for their Lord, when he will return from the wedding; that, when he cometh and knocketh, they may open unto him immediately. Blessed are those servants, whom the Lord when he cometh shall find watching; verily I say unto you, that he shall gird himself, and make them to sit down to meat, and will come forth and serve them. And if he shall come in the second watch, or come in the third watch, and find them so, blessed are those servants.

Immediately before the benediction shall be said these Collects following:—

Almighty God, Giver of all good things, who of thy great goodness hast vouchsafed to accept and take these thy servants into the office of Deacons in thy

Church; make them, we beseech thee, O Lord, to be modest, humble, and constant in their ministration, and to have a ready will to observe all spiritual discipline; that they having always the testimony of a good conscience, and continuing ever stable and strong in thy Son Christ, may so well behave themselves in this inferior office, that they may be found worthy to be called into the higher ministries in thy Church, through the same, thy Son our Saviour Jesus Christ; to whom be glory and honor, world without end. *Amen.*

Prevent us, O Lord, in all our doings, with thy most gracious favor, and further us with thy continual help; that in all our works, begun, continued, and ended in thee, we may glorify thy holy name, and finally, by thy mercy, obtain everlasting life, through Jesus Christ our Lord. *Amen.*

The peace of God, which passeth all understanding, keep your hearts and minds in the knowledge and love of God, and of his Son Jesus Christ our Lord. And the blessing of God Almighty, the Father, the Son, and the Holy Ghost, be among you, and remain with you always. *Amen.*

Laying a Corner-Stone.

490. FORM FOR LAYING THE CORNER-STONE OF A CHURCH.

The Minister, standing near the place where the stone is to be laid, shall say unto the Congregation,—

DEARLY BELOVED, We are taught in the word of God, that, although the heaven of heavens cannot contain the Eternal One, much less the walls of temples made with hands, yet his delight is ever with the sons of men, and that wherever two or three are gathered in his name, there is he in the midst of them. And in all ages his servants have separated certain places for his worship: as Jacob erected a stone in Bethel for God's house; as Moses made a tabernacle in the desert; as Solomon builded a temple for the Lord, which he filled with the glory of his presence before all the people. We are now assembled to lay the corner-stone of a new house for the worship of the God of our fathers. Let us not doubt that he will favorably approve our godly purpose, and let us now devoutly unite in singing his praise, and in prayer for his blessing on this our undertaking.

Let one of the hymns 959–963 *be sung.*

Then shall the Minister say,—

Let us pray.

Most glorious God, the heaven is thy throne and the earth is thy footstool; what house then can be builded for thee, or where is the place of thy rest? Yet, blessed be thy name, O Lord God, that it hath pleased thee to have thy habitation among the sons of men, and to dwell in the midst of the assembly of the saints upon the earth. And now, especially, we render thanks unto thy holy name that it hath pleased thee to put it into the hearts of thy servants to erect in this place a house for thy worship. We thank thee for thy grace which has inclined them to contribute of their substance for the glory of thy name: and we pray thee to continue thy blessing upon their pious undertaking. *Amen.*

May many unite with them in their

holy work, until this habitation of thy house shall be completed, and ready for dedication to thy service, free from all debt or claim of man. *Amen.*

May peace and harmony prevail in the counsels of thy servants, and may no selfish or divided aims find place among them. May the work of this building be completed without hurt or accident to any person. And when thou shalt have prospered the work of their hands upon them, and this house shall be prepared and finished for thy service, grant that all who shall enjoy the benefit of this pious work may show forth their thankfulness by making a right use of it, to the glory of thy blessed name; through Jesus Christ our Lord. *Amen.*

Grant that all who shall hereafter worship thee in the temple here to be builded, may so serve and please thee in all holy exercises of godliness, that in the end they may come to that temple on high, even to the holy places made without hands, whose builder and maker is God. *Amen.*

Hear us, O Lord, for thou art our God in whom we trust. And when we shall cease to pray unto thee on earth, may we, with all those who in like manner have erected such places to thy name, and with all thy saints and redeemed ones, eternally praise thee for all thy goodness vouchsafed unto us here on earth and laid up for us there in heaven. *Amen.*

Accept these our prayers, we beseech thee, for the sake of thy dear Son; and to thee, the only true and living God, Father, Son, and Holy Ghost, be honor, praise, and glory, for ever and ever *Amen.*

Then shall the Minister read the following Psalm, or the Minister and people may read it in alternate verses; the parts in italics to be read by the people.

Psalm cxxxii.

Lord, remember David, and all his afflictions:

How he sware unto the Lord and vowed unto the mighty God of Jacob;

Surely I will not come into the tabernacle of my house, nor go up into my bed;

I will not give sleep to mine eyes, or slumber to mine eyelids,

Until I find out a place for the Lord,

A habitation for the mighty God of Jacob.

Lo, we heard of it at Ephratah: we found it in the fields of the wood.

We will go into his tabernacles: we will worship at his footstool.

Arise, O Lord, into thy rest; thou, and the ark of thy strength.

Let thy priests be clothed with righteousness;

And let thy saints shout for joy.

For thy servant David's sake turn not away the face of thine anointed.

The Lord hath sworn in truth unto David; he will not turn from it;

Of the fruit of thy body will I set upon thy throne.

If thy children will keep my covenant and my testimony that I shall teach them, their children shall also sit upon thy throne for evermore.

For the Lord hath chosen Zion; he hath desired it for his habitation.

This is my rest forever; here will I dwell; for I have desired it.

I will abundantly bless her provision:

I will satisfy her poor with bread.

I will also clothe her priests with salvation:

And her saints shall shout aloud for joy.

There will I make the horn of David to bud:

I have ordained a lamp for mine anointed.

His enemies will I clothe with shame:

But upon himself shall his crown flourish.

The Lesson. 1 Cor. iii, 9–23.

For we are laborers together with God: ye are God's husbandry, ye are God's building. According to the grace of God which is given unto me, as a wise masterbuilder, I have laid the foundation, and another buildeth thereon. But let every man take heed how he buildeth thereupon. For other foundation can no man lay than that is laid, which is Jesus Christ. Now if any man build upon this foundation gold, silver, precious stones, wood, hay, stubble; every man's work shall be made manifest: for the day shall declare it, because it shall be revealed by fire; and the fire shall try every man's work of what sort it is. If any man's work abide which he hath built thereupon, he shall receive a reward. If any man's work shall be burned, he shall suffer loss: but he himself shall be saved; yet so as by fire. Know ye not that ye are the temple of God, and that the Spirit of God dwelleth in you? If any man defile the temple of God, him shall God destroy; for the temple of God is holy, which temple ye are. Let no man deceive himself. If any man among you seemeth to be wise in this world, let him become a fool, that he may be wise. For the wisdom of this world is foolishness with God: for it is written, He taketh the wise in their own craftiness. And again, The Lord knoweth the thoughts of the wise, that they are vain. Therefore let no man glory in men: for all things are yours; whether Paul, or Apollos, or Cephas, or the world, or life, or death, or things present, or things to come; all are yours; and ye are Christ's; and Christ is God's.

Then shall follow the Sermon, or an Address suitable to the occasion, after which the contributions of the people shall be received.

Then shall the Minister, standing by the stone, exhibit to the Congregation a box to be placed in an excavation of the stone. It may contain a copy of the Bible, the Hymn Book, the Discipline, the Church Almanac for the year, Church periodicals of recent date, the names of the Pastor, Trustees, and Building Committee of the Church, with such other documents as may be desired. A list of these may be read, *after which the Minister may deposit the box in the stone and cover it: and the stone shall be laid and adjusted by the Minister, assisted by the builder.*

Then shall the Minister say:—

In the name of the Father, and of the Son, and of the Holy Ghost, we lay this corner-stone for the foundation of a house to be builded and consecrated to the service of Almighty God, according to the order and usages of the Methodist Episcopal Church. *Amen.*

The service may conclude with extemporary prayer, the Lord's Prayer, and the Benediction.

Dedication of a Church.

¶ 491. FORM FOR THE DEDICATION OF A CHURCH.

The Congregation being assembled in the Church, the Minister shall say,—

DEARLY BELOVED; The Scriptures teach us that God is well pleased with those who build temples to his name. We have heard how he filled the temple of Solomon with his glory, and how in the second temple he manifested himself still more gloriously. And the Gospel approves and commends the centurion who built a synagogue for the people. Let us not doubt that he will also favorably approve our purpose of dedicating this place in solemn manner, for the performance of the several offices of religious worship; and let us now devoutly join in praise to his name, that this godly undertaking hath been so far completed, and in prayer for his further blessing upon all who have been engaged therein, and upon all who shall hereafter worship his name in this place.

Let one of the hymns 964–971 *be sung, and extemporary prayer be offered, the Congregation all kneeling.*

Then shall the Minister, or some one appointed by him, read

The First Lesson. 2 Chron. vi, 1, 2, 18–21, 40–42; vii, 1–4.

Then said Solomon, The Lord hath said that he would dwell in the thick darkness. But I have built a house of habitation for thee, and a place for thy dwelling forever.

But will God in very deed dwell with men on the earth? Behold, heaven and the heaven of heavens cannot contain thee; how much less this house which I have built! Have respect therefore to the prayer of thy servant, and to his supplication, O Lord my God, to hearken unto the cry and the prayer which thy servant prayeth before thee: that thine eyes may be open upon this house day and night, upon the place whereof thou hast said that thou wouldest put thy name there; to hearken unto the prayer which thy servant prayeth toward this place. Hearken therefore unto the supplications of thy servant, and of thy people Israel, which they shall make toward this place: hear thou from thy dwellingplace, even from heaven; and when thou hearest, forgive.

Now, my God, let, I beseech thee, thine eyes be open, and let thine ears be attent unto the prayer that is made in this place. Now therefore arise, O Lord God, into thy resting place, thou, and the ark of thy strength: let thy priests, O Lord God, be clothed with salvation, and let thy saints rejoice in goodness. O Lord God, turn not away the face of thine anointed: remember the mercies of David thy servant.

Now when Solomon had made an end of praying, the fire came down from heaven, and consumed the burnt-offering and the sacrifices; and the glory of the Lord filled the house. And the priests could not enter into the house of the Lord, because the glory of the Lord had filled the Lord's house. And when all the children of Israel saw how the fire came down, and the glory of the Lord upon the house, they bowed themselves with their faces to the ground upon the pavement, and worshiped, and praised the Lord, saying, For he is good; for his mercy endureth forever. Then the king and all the people offered sacrifices before the Lord.

The Second Lesson. Heb. x, 19–26.

Having therefore, brethren, boldness to enter into the holiest by the blood of Jesus, by a new and living way, which he hath consecrated for us, through the vail, that is to say, his flesh; and having a high-priest over the house of God; let us draw near with a true heart in full assurance of faith, having our hearts sprinkled from an evil conscience, and our bodies washed with pure water. Let us hold fast the profession of our faith without wavering; for he is faithful that promised; and let us consider one another to provoke unto love and to good works: not forsaking the assembling of ourselves together, as the manner of some is; but exhorting one another: and so much the more, as ye see the day approaching. For if we sin willfully after that we have received the knowledge of the truth, there remaineth no more sacrifice for sins.

Then shall one of the hymns 964–971 be sung; after which the Minister shall deliver a Sermon suitable to the occasion; after which the contributions of the people shall be received.

Then shall the Minister read the following Psalm, or the Minister and the Congregation may read it alternately; the parts in italics to be read by the Congregation.

Psalm cxxii.

I was glad when they said unto me, Let us go into the house of the Lord.

Our feet shall stand within thy gates, O Jerusalem.

Jerusalem is builded as a city that is compact together:

Whither the tribes go up, the tribes of the Lord,

Unto the testimony of Israel, to give thanks unto the name of the Lord.

For there are set thrones of judgment, the thrones of the house of David.

Pray for the peace of Jerusalem:

They shall prosper that love thee.

Peace be within thy walls,

And prosperity within thy palaces.

For my brethren and companions' sakes, I will now say, Peace be within thee.

Because of the house of the Lord our God I will seek thy good.

Then let the Trustees stand up before the altar, and one of them, or some one in their behalf, say unto the Minister,

We present unto you this building, to be dedicated as a church for the service and worship of Almighty God.

Then shall the Minister request the Congregation to stand, while he repeats the following

DECLARATION.

Dearly beloved: It is meet and right, as we learn from the Holy Scriptures, that houses erected for the public worship of God should be specially set apart and dedicated to religious uses. For such a dedication we are now assembled. With gratitude, therefore, to Almighty God, who has signally blessed his servants in their holy enterprise of erecting this church, we dedicate it to his service, for the reading of the Holy Scriptures, the preaching of the word of God, the administration of the holy sacraments, and for all other exercises of religious worship and service, according to the discipline and usages of the Methodist Episcopal

Church. And, as the dedication of the temple is vain without the solemn consecration of the worshipers also, I now call upon you all to dedicate yourselves anew to the service of God. To him let our souls be dedicated, that they may be renewed after the image of Christ. To him let our bodies be dedicated, that they may be fit temples for the indwelling of the Holy Ghost. To him may our labors and business be dedicated, that their fruit may tend to the glory of his great name, and to the advancement of his kingdom. And that he may graciously accept this solemn act, let us pray.

The Congregation kneeling, the Minister shall offer the following prayer :—

O most glorious Lord, we acknowledge that we are not worthy to offer unto thee any thing belonging unto us; yet we beseech thee, in thy great goodness, graciously to accept the dedication of this place to thy service, and to prosper this our undertaking; receive the prayers and intercessions of all those thy servants who shall call upon thee in this house; and give them grace to prepare their hearts to serve thee with reverence and godly fear; affect them with an awful apprehension of thy divine majesty, and a deep sense of their own unworthiness; that so approaching thy sanctuary with lowliness and devotion, and coming before thee with clean thoughts and pure hearts, with bodies undefiled, and minds sanctified, they may always perform a service acceptable to thee, through Jesus Christ our Lord. *Amen.*

Regard, O Lord, the supplications of thy servants, and grant that whosoever shall be dedicated to thee in this house by baptism, may ever remain in the number of thy faithful children. *Amen.*

Grant, O Lord, that whosoever shall receive in this place the blessed sacrament of the body and blood of Christ, may come to that holy ordinance with faith, charity, and true repentance; and being filled with thy grace and heavenly benediction, may, to their great and endless comfort, obtain remission of their sins, and all other benefits of his death. *Amen.*

Grant, O Lord, that by thy holy word, which shall be read and preached in this place, and by thy Holy Spirit grafting it inwardly in the heart, the hearers thereof may both perceive and know what things they ought to do, and may have power and strength to perform the same. *Amen.*

Now, therefore, arise, O Lord, and come unto this place of thy rest, thou and the ark of thy strength. Let thine eye be open toward this house day and night; and let thine ears be ready toward the prayers of thy children which they shall make unto thee in this place: and whensoever thy servants shall make to thee their petitions here, do thou hear them from heaven, thy dwellingplace, the throne of the glory of thy kingdom; and when thou hearest, forgive. And grant, O Lord, we beseech thee, that here and elsewhere thy ministers may be clothed with righteousness, and thy saints rejoice in thy salvation. And may we all, with thy people every-where, grow up into a holy temple in the Lord, and be at last received into the glorious temple above; the house not made with hands, eternal in the heavens. And to the Father, and the Son, and the Holy Spirit, be glory and praise, world without end. *Amen.*

The services to conclude with a Doxology and Benediction.

APPENDIX.

COURSE OF STUDY FOR PREACHERS.

For Admission on Trial.

Candidates must be acquainted with,—

The common branches of an English education.

Ancient History. *Rawlinson.*

Scripture History, Old and New Testament. *Smith.*

History of the United States. *Ridpath.*

History of Methodism. (Abridged.) *Stevens.*

Rhetoric. *Haven.*

Logic. *True.*

Discipline of the Methodist Episcopal Church.

[Read—Wakefield's Theology ; Watson's Life of Wesley ; Whitney's Handbook of Bible Geography ; Foster's Christian Purity ; the Student's Gibbon.]

First Year.

Theological Institutes. *Watson.* (Part I.)

Plain Account of Christian Perfection. *Wesley.*

Church History. *Waddington.*

Homiletics. *Kidder.*

Mental Philosophy. *Upham.*

Written Sermon.

[Read — Wesley's Sermons; Stevens's History of Methodism; New Testament Theology, *Von Oosterzee;* Early Years of Christianity. *Pressensé.*]

Second Year.

Statement and Scripture Proofs of Bible Doctrine.

Theological Institutes. *Watson.*(Part II.)

Baptism. *Hibbard.*

Moral Science. *Wayland.*

Written Sermon.

[Read—Whedon on the Will; Emory's Defense of our Fathers; Porter's Compendium of Methodism; Gaussen's Origin and Inspiration of the Bible; Rawlinson's Historical Evidences; Shedd's Homiletics and Pastoral Theology.]

Third Year.

Theological Institutes. *Watson.* (Parts III and IV.)

Introduction to the New Testament. *Nast.*

Analogy of Natural and Revealed Religion. *Butler.* [*Cummings's Edition.*]

Hand-Book of the Bible. *Angus.*

Logic. *Whately.*

Written Sermon.

[Read—Hagenbach's History of Doctrines; Hurst's History of Rationalism; D'Aubigné's History of the Reformation; Wythe's Agreement of Science and Revelation.]

Fourth Year.

PERSONAL RELIGIOUS LIFE AND HABITS.

1. State your views of the character and source of the Christian life.

2. How may we know that we are partakers of this life?

3. What are the evidences of a divine call to the ministry?

4. State what you consider to be the main duties of the ministerial office, and the necessary qualifications for the discharge of them.

5. By what means may these qualifications be cultivated?

23

6. Give your views of the nature and importance of Pastoral Visitation, and state the amount of attention you give to it.

7. Inform us of your general habits of study.

8. Name all the books you have read each year since your admission on trial in the traveling ministry.

9. How much time do you devote to the study of the Scriptures, and with what method do you study them?

EXAMINATION ON THE BIBLE.

1. In what sense do you consider the Bible to be the word of God, and by what arguments do you sustain your views?

2. Explain what is meant by the phrase "Canon of Scripture."

3. Distinguish between the genuineness, and authenticity, and credibility of a book.

4. Give a synopsis of the argument by which the genuineness of the books constituting our received Canon of the Old Testament is established.

5. Give a synopsis of the argument establishing the genuineness of the books

contained in the received Canon of the New Testament.

6. In what sense do Protestants affirm and Romanists deny that the Scriptures form a complete and infallible rule of faith and practice?

7. State when the authorized version of the Bible appeared, and how it was produced.

8. Give an epitome of the history of the Israelites from the time of the Exodus to the death of Joshua.

9. Recount the leading facts connected with the revolt of the Ten Tribes.

10. Name the great Annual Festivals of the Jews; and also state what they were designed to commemorate, and how they were observed.

11. Name the principal prophets, the periods in which they prophesied, and the particular burdens of their prophecy.

12. Give from the life of our Lord some illustrations of his regard for the Old Testament Scriptures.

13. What predictions relate to Christ, especially to the time of his coming? his character? office? death?

14. Of what periods of the life of our Lord have we historical records? and

over how long a period did his ministry extend?

15. Describe the principal events and localities of his ministry.

16. State the leading facts recorded in the Acts of the Apostles.

17. What is a miracle? In what way do miracles authenticate a divine revelation?

ON THE DOCTRINES OF THE BIBLE.

1. In what manner does the Bible make known the existence of God?

2. What Scripture proof is there of a Trinity of Persons in one Godhead?

3. Enumerate the attributes of God, and give Scripture proofs of each.

4. Give the scriptural doctrine of the Incarnation, and show how it is connected with the Gospel scheme.

5. Give a summary of the Scripture argument for the Divinity of Christ.

6. Give the Scripture proof of the Personality, Divinity, and Work of the Holy Spirit.

7. What was the effect of Adam's sin upon himself? upon his posterity?

8. What is the relation of the vicarious death of Christ to the forgiveness of our sins.

9. State the proofs by which the resurrection of Christ is established.

10. Show the nature and value of Christ's intercession as taught in the Scriptures.

11. What are the doctrine and proof of the Witness of the Spirit ?

12. State concisely the doctrine of Christian perfection as taught by Mr. Wesley, and support it by Scripture proofs.

13. Explain the difference between regeneration or the new birth, and entire sanctification.

14. State the Arminian doctrine respecting the perseverance of the saints, and show its harmony with the Scriptures.

15. State the nature, design, and obligation of Baptism; and the proofs of each.

16. State why baptism of infants should be retained in the Church.

17. What are the phrases used in Scripture to designate the Lord's Supper; what their import ? what the ground of obligation on Christians to observe this sacrament ?

18. State the Romish doctrine of Transubstantiation; also the Lutheran doctrine of Consubstantiation; and give an

outline of the arguments by which each is disproved.

19. How do you prove that the wicked will not be annihilated?

20. State the Scripture doctrine of the resurrection of the body, and give the proofs.

CHURCH ORGANIZATION AND GOVERNMENT.

1. State the different forms of Church government.

2. State the character of the organization in Great Britain; in what respects it differs from, and in what it agrees with, that of the Methodist Episcopal Church in the United States.

3. What are the respective duties and powers of the General Conference and of the Annual and Quarterly Conferences in the Methodist Episcopal Church?

4. What are the peculiar duties and powers vested in the following officers of the Church respectively, namely: Bishops, Presiding Elders, Elders, Deacons, Preachers in Charge, Local Preachers, Stewards, Trustees of Churches, and Class Leaders? and how is the limitation of the power, and the amenability of each for its proper exercise, fixed?

ECCLESIASTICAL HISTORY.

1. Enumerate and describe the principal Jewish sects existing at the time of Christ.

2. Give some account of the early persecutions of the Christians.

3. Mention some circumstances in the state of the world which assisted the early progress of Christianity.

4. State the doctrines of the Gnostics, and show their evil influence upon the early Church.

5. State the chief causes which led to the separation of the Greek from the Latin Church, and the period when it took place.

6. Give an account of the religious state of the world immediately prior to the time of Luther.

7. Give an account of the Great Reformation — the causes that led to it, and the principal characters engaged in it.

8. Give an account of the Reformation in England; also of the Puritans.

9. Give an account of the origin and rise of Methodism in Great Britain, and the leading characters in the Wesleyan movement.

10. How did Methodism take its origin in this country? who were its principal founders? what were the principal characteristics of the movement?

11. What were the circumstances that led to the organization of the Methodist Episcopal Church? what were the time, place, and circumstances under which that organization was effected.

12. State the leading events in the history of the Methodist Episcopal Church since its organization.

[Read—Thomson's Evidences of Revelation; M'Clintock's Methodology; Kidder's Christian Pastorate; Hervey's Christian Rhetoric; Conybeare and Howson's Life and Epistles of St. Paul.]

BOOKS OF REFERENCE—Fleming's Vocabulary of Philosophy; Smith's smaller Classical Dictionary; M'Clintock and Strong's Cyclopædia; Haydn's Dictionary of Dates.

For Local Preachers who are Candidates for Deacons' Orders.

THE BIBLE—DOCTRINES.

The Existence of God—The attributes of God, namely: Unity, spirituality, eternity, omnipotence, ubiquity, omniscience, immutability, wisdom, truth, justice, mercy, love, goodness, holiness; the Trinity in Unity; the Deity of Christ; the humanity of Christ; the union of Deity and humanity; personality and Deity of the Holy Ghost; depravity; atonement; repentance; justification by faith; regeneration; adoption; the witness of the Spirit; growth in grace; Christian perfection; possibility of final apostasy; immortality of the soul; resurrection of the body; general judgment; rewards and punishments.

THE BIBLE—SACRAMENTS.

The sacrament of baptism: its nature, design, obligation, subjects, and mode. The Sacrament of the Lord's Supper: its nature, design, and obligation.

[The examination on the above subjects is to be strictly biblical, requiring the candidates to give the statement of the doctrine and the Scripture proofs. To prepare for this, he should read the Bible by course, and make a memorandum of the texts upon each of these topics as he proceeds.]

SYSTEMATIC DIVINITY

Watson's Institutes, Parts I and II Wesley's Plain Account of Christian Perfection; Fletcher's Appeal.

Church Government: Methodist Discipline.

Common English: English grammar, modern geography.

[Read — Watson's Life of Wesley; Wesley's Sermons; Emory's Defense of our Fathers; Porter's Compendium of Methodism; Merrill on Baptism.]

For Local Preachers who are Candidates for Elders' Orders.

Review of the previous course.

THE BIBLE—HISTORY.

The leading events recorded in the Old and New Testaments.

Systematic Divinity: Watson's Institutes, Parts III and IV.

An Essay or Sermon.

[Read—Stevens's History of Methodism; Ruter's Church History; Binney's Theological Compend.]

[For Course of Study for Local Preachers generally, see pages 391, 392.]

FOR GERMAN PREACHERS.

For Admission on Trial.

Fletcher's Appeal; the Doctrines and Discipline of the M. E. Church, Part I, ¶¶ 1–35; ¶¶ 46–53; Part II, ¶¶ 72–92; ¶¶ 99–148; the Life and Work of John Wesley, as published in German by the Western Book Concern, (Nast's Wesley und seine Mitarbeiter;) the Outlines of Universal History, (Die Weltgeschichte verlegt vom Calwer Verein;) The Outlines of Church History, (Die Kirchengeschichte verlegt vom Calwer Verein;) Elementary Grammar of the German language; we would recommend "Meüwsen's deutsche Sprachlehre in Katechetischer Form."

First Year.

Wesley's Sermons, Vol. I, (Ger. ed.;) Sultzberger's Systematic Theology, Part I; Nast's Introduction to the New Testament, (Ger. ed.,) chap. i, and of chap. ii, § 1–3; Stevens's History of the M. E. Church, Vol. I, (Ger. ed.;) Dr. Kurtz's Sacred History, (Die Hlge. Gchte., imported from Germany;) Wurst's German Grammar, § 1–8, § 43–80, published by the Western Book Concern ; English Grammar, (Ahn's Practischer Lehrang der englishon Sprache, Erster, Cursus;) A written sermon on the conditions of salvation.

Second Year.

Sultzberger's Systematic Theology, Part II; Hare on Justification, (German edition, published by the Western Book Concern;) Wesley's Christian Perfection; Nast's Introduction, chap. ii, § 4, and chap. iii, (German edition;) Stevens's History of the M. E. Church, Vol. II, (German edition, published by the Western Book Concern;) Sauer's Church History, from the Foundation of the Church to Charlemagne, (imported from Germany;) Bishop Baker's Guide in the Administration of Discipline ; Wurst's German Grammar, § 9–42 ; English Grammar, (Ahn's Zweiter Cursus;) a written sermon on baptism.

Third Year.

Nast's Introduction, chap. iv ; Dr. Luthart's Apologetical Discourses, Vol. I, (Apologetische Vortrage, imported from Germany;) Pearson on Infidelity, Part I, chap. i–iii, translated from the English; Sauer's Church History, from Charlemagne to the Reformation; Weber's Universal History, condensed, Parts I and II, (German edition, imported from Germany;) Sultzberger's Systematic Theology, Part III; a written sermon on sanctification.

Fourth Year.

Sultzberger's Systematic Theology, Part IV; Nast's Introduction to the New Testament, chap. v–vii; Dr. Luthart's Apologetical Discourses, Vol. II; Pearson on Infidelity, Part I, chap. iv–vi; Sauer's Church History, from the Reformation to the Present Time; Weber's Universal History, Parts III and IV; a written sermon on the Lord's Supper.

For Local Preachers who are Candidates for Deacons' Orders.

Binney's Theological Compend, translated by Dr. Jacoby; Wesley's Sermons, Vol. I, (German edition;) Fletcher's Appeal; Jacoby's Compendium of Methodism; Nast's Introduction to the New Testament, chap. ii, § 1–3, (German edition;) the Outlines of Universal History, (die Weltgeschichte verlegt vom Calwer Verein;) the Outlines of Church History, (published by the Calwer Verein.)

For Local Deacons, who are Candidates for Elders' Orders.

The Apostolical Creed on the basis of Dr. Lisco; Nast's Introduction, chap. iii, and of chap. iv, § 1, 3, and 4; Stevens's History of the M. E. Church, Vols. I and II; Bishop Baker's Guide in the Administration of Discipline.

MISCELLANEOUS.

---

1. The Right to take Testimony before a Committee, etc.

Testimony taken before a Committee sitting in the case of an accused member of an Annual Conference is to be received as evidence on the trial of said Minister before the Annual Conference.—*Journal*, 1848, p. 126.

2. To whom a Member holding a Certificate is Accountable.

When a member receives a certificate of membership from a Preacher having charge of a Circuit or Station he is responsible for his moral conduct (from the date of his certificate until he joins) to the Society receiving him upon that certificate.—*Journal*, 1848, p. 126.

3. New Testimony not Admissible on Appeal.

In no case of an appeal can new evidence be admitted.—*Journal*, 1860, p. 137.

4. Probationers no Right to Bring Charges.

Question. Has a probationer in our Church the right to prefer charges against a member of our Church?

Answer. He has not.—*Journal*, 1860, p. 228.

5. Status of Members improperly Received or Expelled.

If a Preacher in Charge of any work receive a person into the Church contrary to the Discipline, can the Annual Conference correct the administration, and declare that the person, having been received contrary to Discipline, is therefore not a member?

Answer. No. This question was decided by the General Conference of 1852 by the adoption of the following resolution:

Resolved, That when an Annual Conference decides that a Preacher having charge has received or expelled a member contrary to the Discipline, the decision does not exclude the member so received, but restores the member so expelled.—*Journal*, 1852, p. 73, and *Journal*, 1860, p. 297.

When a member is expelled from the Church, and complaint is made against the administrator to his Annual Conference for maladministration, and the Conference decide that the person was expelled contrary to Discipline, what is the relation of the member expelled from the Church? Does the act of the Annual Conference restore the character of the member, so that the charges on which he was expelled are so annulled that the Preacher may legally give him a letter before said charges are disposed of by trial or withdrawn?

Answer. The act of the Annual Conference does not restore his character, but simply his membership, and when so restored he is placed in the position which he occupied before he was tried; that is, he is an accused member, and hence the Preacher is not at liberty to give him a certificate of membership.—*Journal*, 1860, p. 298.

6. Irregularity in the Reception of a Member is not a Bar to Trial.

May a person who has not been formally received into full connection in the Church, but has for a term of years enjoyed all the privileges of a member, and is supposed by the Preacher in Charge and Society to be a member, plead the fact of his non-reception as a bar to proceedings in case of alleged immorality?

Answer. No.—*Journal*, 1860, p. 298.

7. The Right of Appeal may be Forfeited.

When an expelled member has, by neglect or otherwise, forfeited his *right* to appeal, may a subsequent Quarterly Conference, if it desire to do so, grant him the privilege of an appeal?

Answer. No.—*Journal*, 1860, p. 298.

8. Church Records.

Resolved, That a uniform and thorough mode of keeping Church Records is of great importance, and that we advise careful attention thereto on the part of all our Preachers; and we especially commend to the attention of our people and Preachers the new Church Record published by our Book Agents as admirably adapted to promote this desirable end.—*Journal*, 1864, p. 155.

9. Post-Office Address of Local Preachers.

Resolved, That we recommend to the Annual Conferences that they publish in their Conference Minutes annually the names and post-office addresses of all the Local Preachers within their bounds, designating whether the Preacher be an Elder, Deacon, or only licensed. Also, that when practicable they publish in the Minutes brief obituary notices of our Local Preachers.—*Journal*, 1864, p. 256.

10. Form of Blank for Educational Statistics.

1. Name of institution;* 2. Grade; 3. Location; 4. Name and title of president or principal; 5. When founded; 6. Number of instructors. 7. Whole number of students:—(*a.*) Collegiate, (*b.*) Preparatory, (*c.*) Academic; 8. Number of graduates; 9. Number of graduates in the ministry; 10. Honorary degrees conferred:—(*a.*) A.M., (*b.*) D.D., (*c.*) LL.D.; 11. Value of grounds, build-

* If the institution is open for both sexes, affix a star after the name.

ings, and furniture; 12. Endowment; 13. Volumes in libraries; 14. Value of apparatus; 15. Number of specimens in cabinet; 16. Income from tuition; 17. Income from other sources; 18. Indebtedness; 19. Patronizing Conferences; 20. Time of Commencement, or anniversary exercises.

Resolved, That the Secretaries of the Annual Conferences shall send to the Book Agents at New York a copy of the reports furnished by the Presiding Elders.—*Journal*, 1864, p. 259.

11. Week of Prayer.

Resolved, That we regard the annual observance of the Week of Prayer in concert with the Christian people of other denominations as highly salutary, and an appropriate recognition of the unity of the Church, and a suitable expression of faith in the efficacy of prayer, and well calculated to promote the spirituality, the activity, and prosperity of the Church of Christ.—*Journal*, 1872, p. 230.

12. Who are "Laymen."

Resolved, That in all matters connected with the election of Lay Delegates, the word "Laymen" must be understood to include all the members of the Church who are not members of the Annual Conferences.—*Journal*, 1872, p. 442.

13 Day of Prayer for Colleges.

The General Conference ordered this service to be observed hereafter on the last Thursday in January.—*Journal*, 1872, p. 442.

14. Expenses of General Conference.

Resolved, That the Agents of the Book Concern at New York and Cincinnati be a Committee to estimate, as near as may be, the sum necessary to defray the expenses of the next General Conference, and the expenses of delegates appointed by this General Conference to corresponding bodies, and to report the same to the Board of Bishops by the time of their meeting in the fall of 1878.

Resolved, That the Bishops be authorized to apportion the said amount among the several Conferences, according to their best judgment of their ability to meet the same, and notify the said Conferences of the sum apportioned to them, at their sessions in 1879.

Resolved, That it shall be the duty of

the said Conferences to make arrangements for raising the amount so apportioned, and any Conference failing to do so shall forfeit all claim for the expenses of its delegation.—*Jour.*, 1876, May 12.

15. On Vacancies in General Conference Committees.

Resolved, That when a Minister or Layman shall be elected a member of any General Committee, to wit: The Book Committee, the General Missionary Committee, the Church Extension Committee, or the Freedmen's Aid Committee, he shall reside within the General Conference District that he represents at the time of his appointment. And if for any cause he shall remove beyond the limits of such District, or shall cease to be a member of the Methodist Episcopal Church, his office shall become vacant; and the Bishop having charge of the Conference in which the member may have resided, shall appoint his successor from the same Conference to which the retiring member belonged, or within the bounds of which he resided.—*Jour.*, 1876, May 17.

16. Mixed Conferences.

Resolved, 1. That where it is the general desire of the members of an Annual Conference that there should be no division of such Conference into two or more Conferences, embracing in whole or in part the same territory—and where it is not clearly to be seen that such division would favor or improve the state of the work in any Conference—and where the interests and usefulness of even a minority of the members of such Conference, and of the members of the Churches of such Conference, might be damaged or imperiled by division—it is the opinion of this General Conference that such division should not be made.

Resolved, 2. That whenever it shall be requested by a majority of the white members and also a majority of the colored members of any Annual Conference, that such Conference should be divided into two or more Conferences, it is the opinion of this General Conference that such division should then be made; and in that case the Bishop presiding shall be, and is hereby, authorized to organize a new Conference or Conferences. —*Journal*, 1876, May 29.

17. Use of Tobacco.

Resolved, 1. That we advise all our ministers and members to abstain from the use of tobacco as injurious to both soul and body.

Resolved, 2. That we recommend to the Annual Conferences to require candidates for admission to be free from the habit, as hurtful to their acceptability and usefulness among our people.—*Journal*, 1876, May 29.

18. Temperance.

Resolved, 1. That we are unalterably opposed to the importation, manufacture, and sale of all kinds of distilled, fermented, and vinous liquors, designed to be used as a beverage; and that it is the duty of every member of the Christian Church to discountenance and oppose the evil at all times by voice and vote.

Resolved, 2. That we earnestly protest against the members of our Church giving countenance to the liquor traffic by voting to grant license, or signing the petitions of those who desire license to sell either distilled, or fermented, or vinous liquors, or by becoming bondsmen for persons asking such license, or by renting property to be used as the place in or on which to manufacture or sell such intoxicating liquors.

Resolved, 3. That we are fully convinced of the wisdom and absolute need of total legal prohibition.

Resolved, 4. That we recommend the organization of Juvenile Temperance Societies in all our charges and Sunday-schools.

Resolved, 5. That we recognize the necessity of healthy temperance literature, and therefore recommend the publications of the National Temperance Association of New York to the patronage of our people and Sunday-schools.

Resolved, 6. That we recommend the use of none but pure unfermented juice of the grape on our sacramental occasions.

Resolved, 7. That we gratefully recognize and heartily commend the ministry of the gifted and godly women of the Churches in the work of temperance, and in their holy crusade against the liquor traffic.—*Journal*, 1876, May 29.

19. Form of a Constitution for a Sunday-School.

ART. I. This School shall be called the Sunday-school of ———, auxiliary to the Sunday-School Union of the Methodist Episcopal Church, and connected with the Quarterly Meeting Conference of ——. It shall consist of the Preacher in Charge, the Sunday-school Committee appointed by the Quarterly Conference, the officers, the teachers, and the pupils.

ART. II. The object of this School shall be the promotion of Christian character through the devout and diligent study of the word of God.

ART. III. This School shall be under the supervision of a Sunday-school Board, consisting of the Preacher in Charge, the Sunday-school Committee appointed by the Quarterly Conference, the Superintendent, the Assistant Superintendents, the Secretary, the Treasurer, the Librarian, and the teachers of the school.

ART. IV. The Superintendent shall be nominated and elected by the Sunday-school Board, and approved by the Quarterly Conference at its next session after such election. The other officers of the School shall be elected by the Board annually, by ballot, on ——. The teachers of the School shall be nominated by the Superintendent, with the concurrence of the Pastor, and elected by the Board one month subsequently.

ART. V. Regular meetings of this Board shall be held on ——— of each month, for the transaction of such business as relates to the interests of the School, at which the following order shall be observed: 1. Singing and prayer; 2. Calling roll; 3. Reading minutes; 4. Unfinished business; 5. Reports from Committees; 6. Report from Superintendent; 7. Report from Treasurer; 8. Reports from Librarian concerning the state of the Library, and the number and kind of periodicals taken by the school; 9. Reports from the Pastor and Sunday-school Committee; 10. Reports from the teachers; 11. Miscellaneous.

ART. VI. At all meetings for business ——— shall constitute a quorum.

ART. VII. Special meetings of the Board may be called by the Pastor, the Superintendent, or by any three of the members.

ART. VIII. In case of the withdrawal of officers or teachers from the school they cease to be members of this Board; and the place of any officer or teacher habitually neglecting his or her duty, or being guilty of improper conduct, may be declared vacant by a vote of two thirds of the Board present at any regular or special meeting.

ART. IX. Vacancies in the offices may be filled at any monthly or special meeting, one month's notice having been given of the election.

ART. X. This Constitution shall not be altered except by two thirds of all the members present at a meeting called for that purpose, and such alterations must be in harmony with the provisions of the Discipline of the Methodist Episcopal Church.—*Journal*, 1876, May 31.

20. Bible Study for the Family and Sunday-School.

Resolved, That we cordially approve the course of Bible study for the family and the Sunday-school, adopted in 1872 by the Sunday-school Union of our Church, embodying the Lessons of the International Series, the Catechism of the Church, select passages of Scripture to be committed to memory, and special lessons on the doctrines, usages, and benevolent agencies of the Church.

Resolved, That we urge upon our Pastors the importance of employing this system of Church Lessons in all our Churches, and that we especially insist upon the use of the Catechism by the Pastors, according to the Discipline of the Church, in the family, the Sunday-school, at special meetings, and at public meetings appointed foı that purpose.—*Journal*, 1876, May 31.

21. New Conferences.

1. The Nebraska Conference may, during the next four years, by a vote of two thirds of its members present and voting, with the approval of the Bishop presiding, divide into two Conferences on such a line as may be agreed upon.

2. The North-west Iowa Conference may divide into two Conferences during the coming four years, by setting off Dacotah Territory into a separate Conference, whenever two thirds of the members present and voting shall so agree, and the Bishop presiding shall concur.

3. The Rocky Mountain Conference may divide into two Conferences during the next four years, when two thirds of the members present and voting shall ask for such division, and the presiding Bishop shall concur, on such line as may at the same time be agreed upon.

4. The South-western German Confer-

ence may divide into two Conferences within the coming four years, if two thirds of its members shall so decide, and the presiding Bishop shall concur therewith.

5. Whenever two thirds of the Swedish members, both of the Central Illinois and of the Minnesota Conferences, shall in any one year, at the regular sessions of these respective Conferences, with the concurrence of the said Conferences and of the presiding Bishops, ask to be organized into a separate Conference, their request may be granted, and a Swedish Conference may be organized, within such bounds as may at the same time be agreed upon.

6. The boundary line now dividing between the Indiana and the South-eastern Indiana Conferences may be removed, and the two Conferences merged into one, to be known as the Indiana Conference provided that each of said Conferences shall at its next session, by a majority vote, so agree; and provided also that the respective secretaries of the said Conferences shall give notice of such action to the Board of Bishops, whose concurrence shall be necessary to complete such action.

7. The Bishops may have power during the next four years to transfer the German Churches now in the Louisiana Conference to the Southern German Conference, if they deem it advisable, provided said Churches desire such change.

8. The Bishop having Episcopal supervision of the Conferences in India is authorized to annex the District of Cawnpore to the South India Conference at any time during the next four years; *provided*, the consent of both the Annual Conferences in India to such change of boundaries be first obtained.

9. The Bishops are empowered, at their discretion, to extend the boundaries of the Conference of Norway so as to include Denmark; and in case that be done, the Conference shall be called the Conference of Norway and Denmark.

10. Authority is granted to the Bishops to organize an Annual Conference in Italy before the session of the next General Conference, if they shall deem such action desirable.

11. The new Conferences in foreign lands shall not be organized until one of the Bishops shall be present.—*Journal*, 1876, May 31.

22. Action of General Conference restricting, in certain cases, the Authority of the Agents to pay Drafts of the Bishops.

Whereas, The impression prevails that the support of the Bishops rests upon the Book Concern; and,

Whereas, The Discipline provides for their support by the Church; and,

Whereas, The advance made by the Book Concern to the Episcopal Fund is only a loan for which the General Conference in 1872 promised to make provision: therefore, in order the more clearly to present this matter to the Church, and more certainly to protect the Book Concern,

Resolved, 1. That we insert in paragraph 476 of the Discipline, after the word "charges," the following, namely: "The amount apportioned to each pastoral charge for the support of the Bishops shall be a *pro rata* claim with that of the stationed Preachers and Presiding Elders, and no such preacher or Presiding Elder shall be entitled to his allowance except to the extent to which the claims of the Bishops are met by the Station or District with which he is connected. And it shall be the duty of the Annual Conferences to see that the amounts apportioned to the different pastoral charges are raised and forwarded quarterly, when practicable, to the Book Agents.

Resolved, 2. That the Book Agents at New York and Cincinnati be instructed to loan to the Episcopal Fund such sums as may be required over and above the collections received to meet the drafts of the Bishops for salary and traveling expenses, and for the widows and orphans of deceased Bishops, from the first of June, 1876, to the first of January, 1877. But they shall not increase the above loans to said Fund by any further amount than is necessary to pay the house rent and traveling expenses of the Bishops, which sums shall be returned to the Book Concern as soon as collected for the Episcopal Fund.—*Journal*, 1876, May 30.

23. Expenses of Judicial Conferences.

1. Triers of Appeals shall have their traveling expenses paid from their place of residence to the place where the Judicial Conference shall be held, and also the expenses of their return, computing the distances traveled by the most direct route.

2. It shall be the duty of each member of said Conference in attendance to render to the Secretary of the Conference a detailed account of his traveling expenses, at the time of the meeting of said Conference, and the Secretary shall forward this statement to the Book Agents.

3. The Secretary shall certify to the Bishop presiding the whole amount to be paid for the holding of said Judicial Conference.

4. The Bishop shall draw an order on the Book Concern: if it be in the Eastern department, on the Agents of the Book Concern at New York; if it should be in the Western department, it shall be drawn on the Agents at Cincinnati.

5. Immediately after the receipt of the draft from the Bishops, the Agents shall cause to be sent to each person the

amount which had been certified to them by the Secretary of the Judicial Conference.

6. This provision shall apply also to expenses of Judicial Conferences already held.—*Journal*, 1876, May 31.

24. General Conference Districts.

First District. East Maine, Maine, New England, New Hampshire, Providence, Vermont—6.

Second District. Foochow, Newark New Jersey, New York, New York East, Troy—6.

Third District. East Genesee, Central New York, Northern New York, North India, South India, Western New York, Wyoming—7.

Fourth District. Central Pennsylvania, East Ohio, Erie, Philadelphia, Pittsburgh, North Ohio—6.

Fifth District. Baltimore, Delaware, Florida, Liberia, North Carolina, South Carolina, Virginia, Washington, West Virginia, Wilmington—10.

Sixth District. Central Ohio, Cincinnati, Indiana, Kentucky, Lexington, North Indiana, Ohio, South-east Indiana—8.

Seventh District. Alabama, Arkansas, Central Alabama, Georgia, Holston, Louisiana, Mississippi, Savannah, Tennessee, Texas, West Texas—11.

Eighth District. Central Illinois, Detroit, Michigan, North-west Indiana, Norway, Rock River, Sweden—7.

Ninth District. Des Moines, Minnesota, North-west Iowa, Upper Iowa, West Wisconsin, Wisconsin—6.

Tenth District. Illinois, Iowa, Kansas, Missouri, St. Louis, Southern Illinois, South Kansas—7.

Eleventh District. California, Colorado, Columbia River, Nebraska, Nevada, Oregon, Rocky Mountain, Southern California—8.

Twelfth District. Central German, Chicago German, East German, Germany and Switzerland, North-west German, Southern German, South-west German—7.

25. Book Committee.

District I, AMI PRINCE,
" II, JACOB B. GRAW,
" III, SANFORD HUNT,
" IV, THOMPSON MITCHELL,
" V, L. C. MATLACK,
" VI, F. C. HOLLIDAY,

District VII, WILLIAM BRUSH,
" VIII, J. L. SMITH,
" IX, W. P. STOWE,
" X, W. S. PRENTICE,
" XI, W. B. SLAUGHTER,
" XII, WILLIAM KOENEKE.

LOCAL COMMITTEE AT NEW YORK.

JAMES H. TAFT, GEORGE J. FERRY,
J. B. CORNELL.

LOCAL COMMITTEE AT CINCINNATI.

AMOS SHINKLE, R. A. W. BRUEHL,
C. W. ROWLAND.

26 General Committee on Missions and Church Extension.

District I, JOSEPH CUMMINGS,
" II, JAMES Y. BATES,
" III, ELIPHALET REMINGTON,
" IV, G. W. CHESBRO,
" V, D. H. K. DIX,
" VI, JOSEPH M. TRIMBLE,
" VII, J. J. MANKER,
" VIII, D. F. BARNES,
" IX, BENNETT MITCHELL,
" X, BERNARD KELLEY,
" XI, H. K. HINES,
" XII, C. A. LOEBER.

27. Freedmen's Aid Committee.

Districts.	Ministers.	Laymen.
I,	L. D. BARROW,	A. M. DICKEY,
II,	T. A. GRIFFIN,	J. G. BARNET,
III,	L. C. QUEAL,	E. OCUMPAUGH,
IV,	I. C. PERSHING,	C. AULTMAN,
V,	W. W. FOREMAN,	W. R. JERVAY,
VI,	N. H. PHILLIPS,	W. C. DE PAUW,
VII,	R. W. HAMMETT,	G. BELL,
VIII,	W. A. SMITH,	D. M'WILLIAMS,
IX,	W. HAMILTON,	N. B. MOORE,
X,	J. M. SULLIVAN,	J. B. WEAVER,
XI,	B. F. CRARY,	J. B. M'KEAN,
XII,	J. ROTHWEILER,	G. A. A. VOIGE.

28. Trustees of the Methodist Episcopal Church.

TERM EXPIRES IN 1880.

Ministers: ISAAC W. WILEY, JOSEPH M. TRIMBLE, FERNANDO C. HOLLIDAY. *Laymen:* EDWARD SARGENT, JOHN COCHENOUR, AMOS SHINKLE.—*Journal*, 1872, p. 374.

TERM EXPIRES IN 1884.

Ministers: LUKE HITCHCOCK, WILLIAM H. GOODE, CHARLES W. KETCHAM. *Laymen:* HARVEY DE CAMP, M. B. HAGANS, WILL CUMBACK.—*Journal*, 1876, May 30.

29. Board of Education.

TERM EXPIRES IN 1880.

Ministers: J. W. LINDSAY, T. BOWMAN. *Laymen:* JOHN ELLIOTT, OLIVER HOYT. —*Journal*, 1868, p. 322.

TERM EXPIRES IN 1884.

Ministers: C. A. HOLMES, E. O. HAVEN. *Laymen:* WM. CLAFLIN, F. H. ROOT.—*Journal*, 1872, p. 411.

TERM EXPIRES IN 1888.

Ministers: E. S. JANES, D. P. KIDDER, *Laymen:* C. C. NORTH, J. LONG -*Journal*, 1876, May 30.

30. Course of Study for Local Preachers.

Let candidates for license to preach be examined in the common branches of an English education, and on their general acquaintance with the Bible and the doctrines and usages of the M. E. Church.

First Year.

The Bible—History. Binney's Theological Compend Improved. Discipline of the M. E. Church.

TO BE READ.—Scripture History—Old Testament.—*Smith.* Watson's Life of Wesley. A Hundred Years of Methodism.—*Simpson.*

Second Year.

The Bible—Doctrines. Wakefield's Theology—First Three Books. Christian Baptism.—*Merrill.*

TO BE READ.—Scripture History—New Testament.—*Smith.* History of the United States.—*Ridpath.* Ruter's Church History—one vol., 8vo.

Third Year.

The Bible—Sacraments. Wakefield's Theology—Last Four Books. Christian Perfection—Wesley's Plain Account.

TO BE READ.—Wesley's Sermons, Vol. I. Introduction to the Gospel Records.—*Nast.* D'Aubigné's History of the Reformation, in one vol., 8vo.

Fourth Year.

Review of the whole course. Written sermon.

TO BE READ.—Wesley's Sermons, Volume II. Compendium of Methodism.—*Porter.*

INDEX.

[The figures refer to the numbers of the ¶s.]

INDEX TO APPENDIX.

[The figures at the *end* of the line in *this* Index refer to the pages.]

www.ingramcontent.com/pod-product-compliance
Lightning Source LLC
LaVergne TN
LVHW021149110826
845150LV00005B/1167

* 9 7 8 1 4 2 5 5 4 6 5 7 1 *